The Life of King Henry VIII: All is True
Or

Did My Heart Love til Now?

Hannah Khalil, after William Shakespeare and John Flet

T0046995

methuen | drama

LONDON • NEW YORK • OXFORD • NEW DELHI • SYDNEY

METHUEN DRAMA
Bloomsbury Publishing Plc
50 Bedford Square, London, WC1B 3DP, UK
1385 Broadway, New York, NY 10018, USA
29 Earlsfort Terrace, Dublin 2, Ireland

BLOOMSBURY, METHUEN DRAMA and the Methuen
Drama logo are trademarks of Bloomsbury Publishing Plc

First published in Great Britain 2022

A catalogue record for this book is available from the British Library.

A catalog record for this book is available from the Library of Congress.

ISBN: PB: 978-1-3503-4754-0
ePDF: 978-1-3503-4755-7
eBook: 978-1-3503-4756-4

Series: Modern Plays

Typeset by Mark Heslington Ltd, Scarborough, North Yorkshire

To find out more about our authors and books visit
www.bloomsbury.com and sign up for our newsletters.

The Life of King Henry VIII: All is True – Or Did My Heart Love til Now? originally opened at Shakespeare's Globe, London, on 19 May 2022, with the following cast and creative team.

CAST *(in alphabetical order)*

Jamie Ballard	**Cardinal Wolsey**
Esmonde Cole	**Surrey / Cromwell**
Natasha Cottriall	**Princess Mary**
Janet Etuk	**Anne Bullen**
Adam Gillen	**King Henry VIII**
Debbie Korley	**Woman One / Patience / Elizabeth I**
Kevin McMonagle	**Chamberlain / Gentleman**
Baker Mukasa	**Norfolk / Sands**
Jonah Russell	**Buckingham / Cardinal Campeius**
Anna Savva	**Woman Two / Hope**
Bea Segura	**Queen Katharine**

CREATIVE TEAM

Assistant Director	**Connie Treves**
Co-composer, Orchestrater & Arranger	**Tom Deering**
Co-composer, Songwriter & Lyricist	**Maimuna Memon**
Movement Director	**Aline David**
Casting Director	**Becky Paris**
Costume Supervisor	**Sydney Florence**
Designer	**Georgia Lowe**
Director	**Amy Hodge**
Fight Director	**RC ANNIE: Ruth Cooper-Brown, Rachel Bown-Williams**
Globe Associate, Movement	**Glynn MacDonald**
Globe Associate, Text	**Giles Block**
Voice	**Gurkiran Kaur**
Writer	**Hannah Khalil**

Cast

Jamie Ballard

Jamie recently played Harry Potter in *Harry Potter and the Cursed Child* at the Palace Theatre and Vanya in *Uncle Vanya* at the Sheffield Crucible. His most recent television credits include BBC One's *Three Girls*, Sky Atlantic's *Penny Dreadful* (Season 3) and BBC One's *Ripper Street*.

Previous work at Shakespeare's Globe includes: *The White Devil* (2017) and *Troilus and Cressida* (2009).

Other theatre credits include: *Henry VI Part One*, *The Merchant of Venice*, *Measure for Measure*, *Romeo & Juliet*, *King John*, *Sweet Charity* (Royal Shakespeare Company); *Mother Christmas*, *Missing Dates*, *Japes Too*, *Michael*, *Japes* (Hampstead Theatre); *Ghosts* (Manchester Home); *King John* (The Rose Theatre); *Macbeth* (ATG); *Scenes from an Execution*, *Antigone*, *Emperor & Galilean*, *Some Trace of Her*, *War Horse*, *Saint Joan* (National Theatre); *Written on the Heart*, *Much Ado About Nothing*, *A Midsummer Night's Dream*, *As You Like It* (RSC & West End); *Gloucestershire*, *Thyestes* (Arcola); *Light Shining in Buckinghamshire* (Arcola/Strawberry Vale Productions); *The Devil Inside Him* (National Theatre Wales); *Anjin – The English Samurai* (Horipro/Thelma Holt Productions/RSC); *Hamlet*, *As You Like It*, *Troilus and Cressida* (Tobacco Factory); *The Changeling*, *Macbeth* (Barbican/Tobacco Factory); *The Ark and The Covenant* (BAC) and *The Duchess Of Malfi* (Salisbury Playhouse).

Other television credits include: *Vera* (ITV Studios); *Father Brown*, *Doctors – Fault Lines*, *Doctors*, *The Hollow Crown II* (BBC); *Sons Of Liberty* (Stephen David Entertainment/ History Channel); *The Great Fire* (ITV); *The Crimson Field* (BBC Drama) and *Amnesia* (Ecosse Film/ITV).

Film credits include: *Suffragette* (Gillerd Production Services Ltd.); *X+Y* (Origin Pictures, Minnow Films); *Kittiwakes* (SYFN); *A Poet in New York* (BBC); *The Comedian* (The Bureau) and *Black Death* (Ecosse Films).

Esmonde Cole

Esmonde is a professional actor and voice-over artist. He will soon be seen in the upcoming Russo Brothers si-fi drama *Citadel* (Amazon Studios).

Other theatre credits include: *Macbeth* (Volcano Theatre – Tour); *The Snow Queen* (The Park Theatre); *Learning To Swim* (Criterion Theatre); *Run It Back* (Talawa*); As You Like It* (Putney Arts Theatre); *Market Boy* (Union Theatre) and *Fracture* (Bomb Factory Theatre).

Television credits include: *Ted Lasso* (Apple TV); *The Cleaner* (BBC); *Back* (Channel 4) and *Still So Awkward* (CBBC).

Voice over credits include: *Doctor Who: Master!!* (Big Finish); *Spitting Image* (BritBox); *Warhammer: Adeptus Titanicus* (Warhammer); *Humane* (Big Finish) and *The Offensive* (Stakhanov).

Natasha Cottriall

Natasha Cottriall trained at Mountview Academy.

Theatre credits include: *Family Tree* (Docklands Festival); *The Welkin* (National Theatre); *Future Conditional* (The Old Vic); *Into the Woods* (Royal Exchange, Manchester); *The Buskers Opera* (Park Theatre); *Here Lie the Remains of Mercy* (Theatre Delicatessen); *Beautiful – The Carole King Musical* (Aldwych Theatre); *The Secret Garden* (Theatre by the Lake); *The Selfish Giant* (Vaudeville Theatre); *Oklahoma!* (Grange Park Opera); *The Lovely Bones* (adapted by Bryony Lavery, Tour) and *Anna Bella Eema* (Arcola).

Television credits include: *Vera* (ITV); *Moving On* (BBC); *Grantchester* (ITV) and *Doctors* (BBC1).

Film credits include: *Aladdin* (Disney) and *Canvas 5* (Short Film).

Janet Etuk

Janet Etuk trained on the Acting and Contemporary Theatre course at East 15.

Theatre credits include: *An Improbable Musical* (Royal & Derngate); *TAO of Glass* (Royal Exchange Theatre for MIF Festival/Heath Ledger Theatre for Perth Festival); *Satyagraha* (English National Opera); *The Language Of Kindness* (Shoreditch Town Hall and UK Tour); *Reasons To Stay Alive* (ETT/Sheffield Theatres); *Dinomania* (New Diorama); *LOVE* (National Theatre, Birmingham Rep, UK and European Tour); *Gastronomic* (Norwich Theatre Royal); *The Scar Test* (Soho Theatre); *A Cracked Plaster Sky* (Omnibus Theatre); *The Love I Feel Is Red* (Tobacco Factory) and *Beyond Caring* (The Yard Theatre, National Theatre and Birmingham Rep).

Film credits include: *LOVE* (BBC, Cuba Pictures); *COLD* (Turtle Key Arts); *The Kids Are Alright* (Encounter/FUEL); Mute Film series: *TURN ON* (76 Ltd); *The Souvenir* (The Souvenir Film Ltd) and *Expecting* (Cestoda Productions). Writing credits include: *Mkpa Mbiet* (Southwark Playhouse, Arcola and Oval Theatre); *The Coconut Series* (Alchemist's 'Writers On Hold' Online Festival) and *Kim* (Arcola Theatre, 'Today I'm Wiser' Festival).

Directing credits include: *Blue Beneath My Skin* (Bunker Theatre); *One For Sorrow* (Co-direction for Blue Elephant Theatre); *Unstable Table's Diary Entries* (Co-direction for Notting Hill Gate Cinema) and *Catnip* (Co-direction for Arts Theatre London).

Adam Gillen

Adam has worked extensively on stage and screen; 2019 gained Adam an Olivier nomination for his performance in *Killer Joe* (Trafalgar Studios) for best supporting actor, prior to which he garnered fantastic reviews for his role as Mozart in Michael Longhurst's production of Peter Shaffer's *Amadeus* at the National Theatre.

_vious work for Shakespeare's Globe includes: *Romeo &
Juliet* (2021).

Theatre credits include: *Radio* (Arcola); *Killer Joe* (Trafalgar
Studios); *Amadeus* (National Theatre); *Wendy and Peter* (RSC);
Lotty's War (Tour/Ambassadors); *Lee Harvey Oswald*
(Finborough); *School for Scandal* (Barbican); *The Door Never
Closes* (Almeida); *For King and Country* (Plymouth TR & Tour/
ACT); *A Taste of Honey* (Royal Exchange Manchester); *Proper
Clever* (Liverpool Playhouse); *The Good Soul of Szechuan*
(Young Vic); *The Lion's Mouth* (Royal Court); *War and Peace*
(Royal Court/Latitude Fest) and *The Five Wives of Maurice
Pinder* (National Theatre).

Television credits include: Dave Spud, *Benidorm* (series 4–10)
and *Miss Wright* (ITV); *Prisoners' Wives* (BBC/Tiger Aspect);
Way to Go, *The Gemma Factor* (BBC 3); *Fresh Meat* (Channel 4/
Objective Productions); *This is Jinsy* (Sky Atlantic) and *Just
William*, *The Sarah Jane Adventures*, *Oliver Twist* (BBC).

Film includes: *Vita and Virginia* (Mirror Productions); *Funny
Cow* (Gizmo Films); *We are the Freaks* (104 Films); *Age of
Heroes*, *4,3,2,1* and *Hippie Hippie Shake* (Working Title Films).

Debbie Korley

Debbie has appeared in leading roles with the Royal
Shakespeare Company.

Previous theatre credits include: *The Fall of The House of
Usher* (Ruhrtriennale International Festival/Burg Theater-
Vienna); *The Whip, A Museum in Baghdad, Tamburlaine, Timon
of Athens, Little Eagles, Morte D'Arthur, Grain Store, Romeo and
Juliet, Hamlet, American Trade, King Lear, As You Like It* (RSC);
Comedy of Errors (RSC/Told by an Idiot); *Acceptance*
(Hampstead Theatre); *Cargo* (Arcola); *Beowulf* (Unicorn
Theatre); *King Lear* (Talawa/Manchester Royal Exchange/
Birmingham Rep); *Boi Boi is Dead* (Leeds Playhouse/Watford
Palace Theatre); *Coram Boy* (National Theatre); *A Matter of
Life and Death* (Kneehigh/National Theatre); *Prurience*,

Welcome To The Home (Southbank Centre); *The Residents* (Albany Theatre/Teatro Vivo); *Too Clever By Half* (Manchester Royal Exchange/Told By An Idiot); *Black Jesus* (Finborough Theatre); *Feathers in the Snow* (National Theatre Studio); *Cinderella* (Theatre Royal Stratford East); *Aida* (Royal Albert Hall); *Whistle Down the Wind* (West End/Tour); *Sick* (Almeida) and *Ten Suitcases* (Drill Hall).

Television credits include: *Delicious* (Bandit Television/SKY); *Holby City*, *Casualty*, *Doctors*, *Holy Smoke*, *Green Balloon Club* (BBC); *Night and Day* (Granada) and *Night Fever* (Five).

Film credits include: *King Lear* (Saffron Cherry TV/BBC); *The One's Below* (Cuba/Tigerlily) and *I Called You* (Double Yellow Productions).

Radio credits include: *The Archers*, *Murmuration*, *The No. 1 Ladies' Detective Agency*, *Home Front*, *What Really Happened in The Nineties: Race* (BBC 4); *Selling Dreams* (Story Glass/ETT); *The Eighth of March – Protectors Of Time: Prism and Gallifrey – Time War: Volume 4* (Big Finish), and a season with the BBC Radio Rep Company.

Kevin McMonagle

Kevin recently performed in *Best of Enemies* at the Young Vic. This is Kevin's debut at Shakespeare's Globe.

Previous theatre credits include: *After Life* (National Theatre/Headlong); *Witness For The Prosecution* (London County Hall); *A Midsummer Night's Dream* (Bridge Theatre); *Mother Courage And Her Children* (Royal Exchange Theatre and Headlong); *The Rise And Fall Of Little Voice* (The Park Theatre); *People, Places and Things* (Headlong/National Theatre/West End/St. Ann's Warehouse, Brooklyn NYC); *Junkyard* (Headlong); *The Tempest* (The Print Room at the Coronet); *The Divided Laing*, *Pieces of Vincent* (Arcola Theatre); *No Nothing* (Lemon Tree/Oran Mor); *A Doll's House* (National Theatre of Scotland); *Twelfth Night*, *The Tempest*, *The Comedy of Errors*, *Richard III* (RSC); *Ambulance*, *Thyestes*,

Ladybird, Kin (Royal Court) and *The Family Reunion* (Donmar Warehouse).

Television credits include: *New Tricks* (BBC); *Krakatoa – The Last Days* (BBC Science); *Quite Ugly One Morning* (Clerkenwell Films); *Rose and Maloney* (Company Pics); *Rebus* (SMG); *Blue Murder* and *Bramwell* (Carlton Television).

Film credits include: *Greenfingers* (Westgrip).

Baker Mukasa

Baker trained at the Royal Central School of Speech and Drama. He is a 2022 Ian Charleson Award nominee for his performance in *The Comedy of Errors* (RSC).

Previous theatre credits include: *The Comedy of Errors, The Winter's Tale, Troy Story, Swingin' the Dream and Festive Tales* (RSC); *The Last King of Scotland* (Sheffield Crucible); *Peter Pan* (Hull Truck); *Tina the Musical* (Aldwych Theatre, West End); *The Hartlepool Monkey* (Fuel/Stratford Circus Arts Centre, UK Tour); *The Beggar's Opera* and *Alice in Wonderland* (Storyhouse Chester) and *Beasty Baby* (Theatre Rites, UK Tour).

Jonah Russell

Jonah is from Nottingham.

Previous theatre credits include: *My Brilliant Friend, Pains of Youth, Waves, Women of Troy, Attempts on her Life, The Seagull* and *War Horse Prom* (National Theatre); *Suzy Stork* (Gate Theatre); *Lady Chatterley's Lover, Romans In Britain* (Sheffield Crucible & ETT); *Of Mice and Men* (Birmingham Rep); *Hood* (Theatre Royal Nottingham); *The Mikvah Project* (The Yard); *A View From the Bridge, Kursk* (Young Vic); *Clytemnestra* (Sherman Cymru); *Yerma* (West Yorkshire Playhouse); *Small Hours* (Hampstead Theatre) and *Waves* (Duke Theatre, New York).

Television credits include: *La Fortuna* (Moviestar+, AMC); *Hatton Garden, Midsomer Murders, Lucy Sullivan is Getting*

Married, *The Bill* (ITV); *Hollow Crown II*, *Holby City*, *EastEnders*, *Doctors*, *D-Day* (BBC); *The Borgias* (Showtime); *24: Live Another Day* (Fox); *Green Wing*, *Melissa* (Channel 4) and *Hidden City* (Hallmark).

Film credits include: *Lady Chatterley's Lover* (Netflix); *1917* (Amblin); *Dark River* (Film 4); *'71* (Warp Films); *Queen and Country* (Merlin Films); *Kursk* (Fuel); *What a Girl Wants* (Warner Bros) and *Dog Eat Dog* (Tiger Aspect).

Radio credits include: *Births, Deaths and Marriages* (Radio 4).

Anna Savva

Anna trained at The London Academy of Music and Dramatic Art (LAMDA) and was a *Time Out* Best Actress Nominee for her performance as Frida Kahlo in *Frida & Diego*.

Previous theatre credits include: *Jude* (Hampstead Theatre); *The Wedding Party* (One-woman play at the Ohrid Festival Macedonia); *The Dybbuk* (NY Fringe Festival – Theater for the New City); *Enduring Freedom* (Finborough); *The Battle of Green Lanes* (Theatre Royal, Stratford East); *The Tunnel* (Edinburgh Festival, Hill Street Theatre); *A Midsummer Night's Dream* (Manchester Royal Exchange); *Frida & Diego* (Red Shift Theatre – *Time Out* nomination for Best Actress); *Kvetch* (West Yorkshire Playhouse); *Salome* (Glasgow Citizens); *A View from the Bridge* (Liverpool Playhouse); *The Four Horsemen of the Apocalypse* (Glasgow Citizens); *Measure For Measure* (Arcola); *The Snow Queen* (Theatr Clywd); *Beauty and the Beast* (Manchester Library Theatre); *The House of Bernarda Alba* (Shaw Theatre); *Hot Fudge & Ice Cream* (Manchester Contact Theatre); *Blood Wedding* (Leicester Haymarket); *Hiawatha* (Sheffield Crucible); *Carmen* (Derby Playhouse) and *Macbeth* (Cherub Theatre Company).

Television credits include: *The Durrells*, *Law & Order UK* (ITV); *Casualty*, *Yo Picasso*, *Drowning in the Shallow End*, *Silent Witness* (BBC); *Genius: Picasso* (Fox Television); *Tyrant* (Fox 21 for FX); *Planespotting*, *Family* (Granada Television); *London's Burning* (Granada Television); *The Chief* (Anglia Television); *Minder* (Thames TV) and *Sharpe's Honour* (Palace Pictures).

Film credits include: *The Correspondence* (Paco Cinematografica); *Exodus* (Fox UK); *The Cut* (Pandora Film); *Salvation Has No Name* (Delaval Film); *O Holy Ghost, The Horror of the Dolls* (Davey Inc Films); *The Quiet Assassin*, *Akamas* (AmaFilms); *Restoration* (Oxford Films) and *Grandma's Funeral*.

Bea Segura

Bea trained at the Institut del Teatre in Barcelona, and at HB Studio in New York. She has enjoyed a successful career in Spain in theatre, film and television.

Previous theatre credits include: *Bonus Track* (Teatre Lliure); *Much Ado about Nothing* (National Theater of Barcelona); *Skin in Flames* (Park Theater); *Blackbird* (Teatre Lliure); *Orestíada* (Teatro Español); *Mourning becomes Electra* (Teatro Español); *El Cuerdo loco* (Teatro en Tránsito) and *The Learned Ladies* (Teatre Romea).

Television credits include: *The Minions of Midas* (Netflix); Hernán (Amazon); *What the future holds* (Movistar); *Monteperdido, la caza* (TVE); *Moebius* (Tv3); *Alba* (Antena3); *Cites* (TVE); *The Sun Trap* (BB1); *Hospital Central* (Telecinco); *Habitaciones Cerradas* (TVE); *Siete Vidas* (telecinco) and *El Comisario* (Telecinco).

Film credits: *Malasaña 32* (Warner Bros); *Insensibles* (Canal +); *Hierro* (Älvaro Agustín Jesús de la Vega) and *Salvador Puig Antich* (Media Pro).

On stage, Bea was nominated for Best Actress in the Premis Butxaca and shortlisted for the Premios Max (the Catalan and Spanish equivalents of the Oliviers) in 2013 for her portrayal of Una in David Harrower's *Blackbird* at the Teatre Lliure, Barcelona, directed by the legendary Lluis Pasqual.

In 2013, she was nominated for Best Actress at the Monte Carlo International Television Festival for Tornarem, which was itself nominated for Best Television Miniseries at the festival and won Best Television Miniseries at the Gaudi Awards (the Catalan equivalent of the BAFTAs).

Creatives

Aline David

Aline David's work in theatre includes: *The Arrival* (Bush Theatre); *A Taste of Honey*, *Barber Shop Chronicles*, *Romeo and Juliet*, *Emil and the Detectives*, *Antigone*, *The Kitchen*, *Greenland* and *Our Class* (National Theatre); *The Brothers Size*, *Dutchman*, *Eurydice*, *Elektra*, *Parallel Macbeth*, *The Invisible Woman* and *Playsize* (Young Vic); *Dance Nation* and *The House of Bernarda Alba* (Almeida); *Macbeth* and *The Merchant of Venice* (RSC); *Gone Too Far!* and *Wanderlust* (Royal Court); *The Iphigenia Quartet* and *How to be Another Woman* (Gate, Notting Hill); *First Love is the Revolution* (Soho Theatre); *Romeo and Juliet*, *A Taste of Honey*, *Alice* (Sheffield Crucible); *Of Mice and Men* (Birmingham Rep); *Looking for Yogurt* (Birmingham Studio); *Romeo and Juliet*, *Women Beware Women*, *Antony & Cleopatra*, *Much Ado About Nothing*, *Troilus and Cressida* and *Handel and the First Messiah* (Shakespeare's Globe); *Proof* (Menier Chocolate Factory); *Waiting for Godot* (West Yorkshire Playhouse); *1984*, *Macbeth* and *The Mighty Waltzer* (Royal Exchange); *A Christmas Carol* (Sherman, Cardiff); *The Owl and the Pussycat* (Royal Opera House Olympic Project); *Working* (Royal Academy of Music); *Nothing* (Glyndebourne Opera / Den Jyske Opera) and *Daphne* (La Monnaie, Belgium).

Tom Deering

Tom studied at Goldsmiths College (University of London) and The Royal Academy of Music.

As a music supervisor/orchestrator/conductor, projects include: *Abomination: A DUP Opera* (Belfast Ensemble/Conor

egents Park Open Air Theatre);
Edge (Sheffield Crucible*); On The Town*
en Air Theatre); *Jesus Christ Superstar*
pen Air Theatre Lyric Opera Chicago & US
ning Man (Bristol Old Vic/Trafalgar Studios);
ational Theatre); *In the Heights* (King's Cross
uthwark Playhouse) and *The Boy in the Dress*
kespeare Company).

*uposer: The Public Administration and Constitutional
Committee Takes Oral Evidence on Whitehall's Relationship
Kids Company* (Donmar Warehouse); *Pity* (Royal Court)
Little Red Riding Hood (Drew McOnie).

Maimuna Memon

Maimuna is a Lancashire-born actor, musician and composer.

Maimuna is Co-Founder and Resident Composer of Wildcard Theatre Company. She wrote the music and lyrics for *Electrolyte* (a gig theatre piece which had a sell-out run at the Edinburgh Fringe 2018/19 and won the Scotsman Mental Health Award), *Nine Lessons and Carols* at the Almeida Theatre and *Welcome To Iran* for the National Theatre and Stratford East (cancelled due to the pandemic but then adapted for BBC Radio 3). She has been commissioned by the Bush Theatre and Bolton Octagon for her new musical *Sparrow Girl*, which is currently in development. She is also bringing her new concept album musical *Manic Street Creature* to the Edinburgh Fringe Festival this year.

Maimuna signed a record deal last year and her first EP is due to be released some time in the summer.

Sydney Florence

Previous work at Shakespeare's Globe includes: *A Midsummer Night's Dream*, *Women Beware Women*, *Love's Labour's Lost*, *All's*

Well That Ends Well, *Lions and Tigers*, *All the Angels*, *The Merchant of Venice*, *The Two Gentlemen of Verona*, *Holy War* *The Comedy of Errors*, *The Taming of the Shrew* and *Much A. About Nothing*.

Other theatre credits include: *Appropriate*, *[BLANK]* (Donmar); *Tree* (Young Vic/MIF); *Our Town, A Tale of Two Cities* (Regent's Park Open Air); *Agrippina* (Grange Park Festival); *Pah-La, Disconnect, Wanderlust* (Royal Court); *Froze* (Theatre Royal Haymarket); *Witness for the Prosecution* (County Hall); *They Drink it in the Congo, Ruined, The Chain Play* (Almeida); *Kursk* (Young Vic); *The Bomb, Stones in His Pockets, Broken Glass, The Great Game: Afghanistan, Women, Power and Politics, Greta Garbo Came to Donegal, Not Black and White season: Cat B, Carpe Diem* and *Detaining Justice, Radio Golf, Let There be Love, Doubt, Called to Account, Fabulation* (Tricycle), *Shakespeare In Love, Abigail's Party* (Theatre Royal Bath); *The Country Wife, Mogadishu, The Comedy of Errors* (Royal Exchange, Manchester); *Approaching Empty* (Kiln); *Sleeping Beauty, Room, The Bubbly Black Girl Loses Her Chameleon Skin* (Theatre Royal Stratford East); *Kiss of the Spider Woman* (Menier Chocolate Factory); *The Secret Garden* (Theatre by the Lake, Keswick); *The Mentor, Half Life, Forever Yours, Mary Lou, Monsieur* Popular (Ustinov Theatre, Bath); *Baddies, Jeremee, Hartleby and Ooglemoore, The Nutcracker, Snowchild, The Velveteen Rabbit, Edward The Fifth* (Unicorn) and *Realism, Fit and Proper People, Piranha Heights, This Isn't Romance, Shraddha, The Diver, The Christ of Coldharbour Lane* (Soho Theatre).

Georgia Lowe

Georgia trained on the Motley Theatre Design course and was a Linbury Prize for Stage Design finalist 2011 and trainee Designer for the RSC.?

Design credits include: *All Of Us, Dick Wittington, Mr Gum and the Dancing Bear – the Musical!* (National Theatre); *The Contingency Plan, Anna Karenina* (Crucible Theatre); *Missing*

Julie (Theatr Clwyd); *Klippies* (Young Vic); *The Twits* (Unicorn Theatre digital); *Macbeth* (The Globe); *Plenty?* (Chichester, Festival Theatre); *Equus* (English Touring Theatre/West End); *Cock?* (Chichester, Minerva Theatre); *?A Streetcar Named Desire?* (Nuffield Theatre/English Touring Theatre); *?An Octoroon?* (National Theatre/Orange Tree Theatre); *Othello?* (Tobacco Factory/English Touring Theatre); *?The Twits?* (Leicester Curve/Tour); *The Night Watch?* (Royal Exchange); *Yen?* (Royal Court/Royal Exchange) and *Pomona?* (National Theatre/Royal Exchange/Orange Tree Theatre).

Amy Hodge

Amy Hodge is an Olivier Nominated theatre and film director.

Previous work for Shakespeare's Globe includes: *Women Beware Women* (2020)

Previous theatre directing credits include: *Mr Gum and The Dancing Bear by Andy Stanton* (National Theatre); *Mother Courage and Her Children* by Bertolt Brecht, adapted by Anna Jordan (Royal Exchange/Headlong); *Meek* by Penny Skinner (Birmingham Rep/Headlong); *Boys Will Be Boys* by Melissa Bubnic (Bush/Headlong) and her first piece of dance *7–75* which she conceived and directed (The Place).

Amy has recently directed 7 short films for *The Guardian* newspaper about the EU and is currently developing her first Virtual Reality Film about the experience of Dementia for the National Theatre.

She was Associate Director at Headlong (2015–18), Studio Associate at The National Theatre (2012–13) and recipient of The Jerwood Directors Award 2008.

RC ANNIE

RC-ANNIE Ltd, established in 2005 by Rachel Bown-Williams and Ruth Cooper-Brown, is the UK's leading Dramatic Violence Company.

Previous work at Shakespeare's Globe: *As You Like It* (Globe on Tour), *Romeo and Juliet*, *Playing Shakespeare with Deutsche Bank – Macbeth, Macbeth, Emilia, Othello, The Secret Theatre, Boudica, Lions and Tigers*; *Much Ado About Nothing*; *Twelfth Night, Comus* and *Imogen*.

Other theatre credits include: *Henry VI Rebellion, Henry VI Wars of the Roses, Henry VI Part 1 Rehearsal Room Project, King John, Measure for Measure, As You Like It, The Taming of the Shrew, Tartuffe, The Duchess of Malfi, Salome & Snow in Midsummer* (RSC); *Theodora* (Royal Opera House); *Persuasion* (Rose Theatre Kingston); *2:22 A Ghost Story* (West End); *The Play What I Wrote* (Birmingham Rep & Tour); *The Life of Pi* (Wyndham Theatre); *Blue/Orange* (Theatre Royal Bath); *Beauty and the Beast* (Theatr Clwyd); *'Night Mother* (Hampstead Theatre); *East is East* (Birmingham Rep/National Theatre/Chichester Festival Theatre); *Once Upon A Time in Nazi Occupied Tunisia* (Almeida Theatre); *The Welkin, Three Sisters, Anna, When We Have Sufficiently Tortured Each Other, Common, Ugly Lies the Bone, Peter Pan, The Threepenny Opera, The James Plays* (co-production with National Theatre of Scotland and Edinburgh International Festival); *Cleansed* (National Theatre); *The Prince of Egypt* (Dreamworks at The Dominion Theatre); *A Monster Calls* (Old Vic Productions National Tour); *Alone in Berlin* (Royal and Derngate); *[BLANK]* (Donmar Warehouse); *Macbeth* (Chichester Festival Theatre); *Hedda Tesman* (Headlong/Chichester Festival Theatre/The Lowry); *The King of Hell's Palace* (Hampstead Theatre); *Peter Pan* (National Theatre); *Troubadour White City Theatre*; *Noises Off* (Lyric Hammersmith & West End); *The Night of the Iguana* (Noel Coward Theatre); *Plenty* (Chichester Festival Theatre); *Hobson's Choice* (Manchester Royal Exchange); *King Hedley* (Theatre Royal Stratford East); *The*

Little Matchgirl; (Bristol Old Vic / Shakespeare's Globe); *A Very, Very, Very Dark Matter* (The Bridge Theatre); *Wise Children* (Wise Children & The Old Vic); *Company* (Elliot Harper Productions at The Gielgud Theatre); *Europe* (Leeds Playhouse; God of *Carnage, The Price, Switzerland, Dusty* (Theatre Royal Bath) and *A Monster Calls, Woyzeck* (Old Vic).

Ruth Cooper-Brown

Theatre credits for Shakespeare's Globe include: *Macbeth, Emilia, Othello, The Secret Theatre, Boudica, Lions and Tigers, Much Ado About Nothing; Twelfth Night, The White Devil, Comus* and *Imogen.*

Other theatre credits include: *The Welkin, Three Sisters, Anna, When We Have Sufficiently Tortured Each Other, Common, Ugly Lies the Bone, Peter Pan, The Threepenny Opera, The James Plays* (co-production with National Theatre of Scotland and Edinburgh International Festival); *Cleansed* (National Theatre); *The Prince of Egypt* (Dreamworks at The Dominion Theatre); A Monster Calls (Old Vic Productions National Tour); *Alone in Berlin* (Royal and Derngate); *[BLANK]* (Donmar Warehouse); *Macbeth* (Chichester Festival Theatre); *Hedda Tesman* (Headlong/Chichester Festival Theatre/The Lowry); *King John, Measure for Measure, As You Like It, The Taming of the Shrew, Tartuffe, The Duchess of Malfi, Salome & Snow in Midsummer* (RSC); *The King of Hell's Palace* (Hampstead Theatre); *Peter Pan* (National Theatre); *Troubadour* (White City Theatre); *Noises Off* (Lyric Hammersmith & West End); *The Night of the Iguana* (Noel Coward Theatre); *Plenty* (Chichester Festival Theatre); *Wife* (Kiln Theatre); *Hobson's Choice* (Manchester Royal Exchange); *King Hedley* (Theatre Royal Stratford East); *The Little Matchgirl*; (Bristol Old Vic / Shakespeare's Globe); *A Very, Very, Very Dark Matter* (The Bridge Theatre); *Wise Children* (Wise Children & The Old Vic); *Company* (Elliot Harper Productions at The Gielgud Theatre); *Europe* (Leeds Playhouse), *God of Carnage, The Price, Switzerland, Dusty*

(Theatre Royal Bath); *A Monster Calls, Woyzeck* (Old Vic); *Hogarth's Progress, My Brilliant Friend* (Rose Theatre Kingston); *The Village* (Theatre Royal Stratford East); *Girl on a Train, Sunshine on Leith, The Lion, The Witch and The Wardrobe, Barnbow Canaries, Great Expectations, Richard III* (West Yorkshire Playhouse) and *A Clockwork Orange* (Liverpool Everyman).

Rachel Bown-Williams

Theatre credits for Shakespeare's Globe include: *Macbeth, Emilia, Othello, The Secret Theatre, Boudica, Lions and Tigers, Much Ado About Nothing; Twelfth Night, The White Devil, Comus* and *Imogen.*

Other theatre credits include: *The Welkin, Three Sisters, Anna, When We Have Sufficiently Tortured Each Other, Common, Ugly Lies the Bone, Peter Pan, The Threepenny Opera, The James Plays* (co-production with National Theatre of Scotland and Edinburgh International Festival), *Cleansed* (National Theatre); *The Prince of Egypt* (Dreamworks at The Dominion Theatre); *A Monster Calls* (Old Vic Productions National Tour); *Alone in Berlin* (Royal and Derngate); *[BLANK]* (Donmar Warehouse); *Macbeth* (Chichester Festival Theatre); *Hedda Tesman* (Headlong/Chichester Festival Theatre/The Lowry); *King John, Measure for Measure, As You Like It, The Taming of the Shrew, Tartuffe, The Duchess of Malfi, Salome, Snow in Midsummer* (RSC); *The King of Hell's Palace* (Hampstead Theatre); *Peter Pan* (National Theatre); *Troubadour* (White City Theatre); *Noises Off* (Lyric Hammersmith & West End); *The Night of the Iguana* (Noel Coward Theatre); *Plenty* (Chichester Festival Theatre); *Wife* (Kiln Theatre); *Hobson's Choice* (Manchester Royal Exchange); *King Hedley* (Theatre Royal Stratford East); *The Little Matchgirl*; (Bristol Old Vic / Shakespeare's Globe); *A Very, Very, Very Dark Matter* (The Bridge Theatre); *Wise Children* (Wise Children & The Old Vic); *Company* (Elliot Harper Productions at The Gielgud Theatre); *Europe* (Leeds Playhouse) *God of Carnage, The Price,*

Switzerland, Dusty (Theatre Royal Bath); *A Monster Calls, Woyzeck* (Old Vic); *Hogarth's Progress, My Brilliant Friend* (Rose Theatre Kingston); *The Village* (Theatre Royal Stratford East); *Girl on a Train, Sunshine on Leith, The Lion, The Witch and The Wardrobe, Barnbow Canaries, Great Expectations, Richard III* (West Yorkshire Playhouse) and *A Clockwork Orange* (Liverpool Everyman).

Glynn MacDonald

Glynn trained in the Alexander Technique in 1972. She is past Chairman of The Society of Teachers of the Alexander Technique (STAT).

She has worked in the Actors Centre and the Field Day Theatre Company in Ireland, Dramaten in Stockholm, Norskspillersforbund in Norway, Holback Engstheatre in Denmark, Bremen Opera Company in Germany and in Poland, Switzerland, Japan, Australia and the USA.

Since 1997 she has been resident Director of Movement at Shakespeare's Globe on all theatre productions and has been a core member of the Globe Education Faculty in their Acting and Training programmes. In the Globe to Globe Festival 2012, she worked with the 37 international companies who brought productions of Shakespeare's plays in their own language to the Globe stage.

In 2002 she directed *Transforming September 11th* at the Linbury Studio, Royal Opera House for Peace Direct.

She shared the Sam Wanamaker Award with Giles Block in 2011 for services to the Globe. In 2012 she was awarded the François Florent Prize in Paris. Glynn is a Faculty Member for 'Arts and Passion-Driven Learning' at Harvard University.

Giles Block

Giles has led the text work at Shakespeare's Globe since 1999, and to date has been involved in over 100 productions. Directing work for Shakespeare's Globe includes: *Antony and Cleopatra, Hamlet* and *Troilus and Cressida*.

Posts include: Associate Director at Ipswich Theatre (1974 – 77), Staff Director at The National Theatre (1977 – 81) and Director of Platforms at The National Theatre (1981 – 84). Other theatre direction includes: *The Fawn, She Stoops to Conquer (National Theatre); Macbeth, The Cherry Orchard, King Lear, Richard III, Hamlet, Skylight* and *Vincent in Brixton* (Shochiku Company, Japan). In 2000 the Association of Major Theatres of Japan recognised Giles for services to the Japanese Theatre. In recent years, Giles has directed *The Tempest, Henry V* and *The Comedy of Errors* at The Blackfriars Theatre in Virginia.

Giles is the author of Speaking the Speech – An Actor's Guide to Shakespeare. In 2011, Giles, together with Glynn MacDonald, was given the Sam Wanamaker Award for services to the Globe.

Gurkiran Kaur

Gurkiran Kaur is a voice, accent and dialect coach from London.

Training: She received her BA in Drama and Theatre Studies from Royal Holloway, University of London before training as an actor at The Bridge Theatre Training Company and has an MA in Voice Studies from The Royal Central School of Speech and Drama.

Coaching: credits include *Extinct* at Theatre Royal Stratford East; *Queens of Sheba* at Soho Theatre; *NW Trilogy* a trio of plays at The Kiln; *How To Save The Planet When You're A Young Carer And Broke* at The Roundhouse; *Best of Enemies* at The Young Vic; *Red Pitch* at The Bush Theatre, and *The Good Karma Hospital* for Tiger Aspect Productions.

Hannah Khalil

Hannah Khalil is Resident Writer at the Globe 2022. Her stage plays include an adaptation of Hans Christian Anderson's *The Fir Tree* (Shakespeare's Globe); *A Museum in Baghdad* (Royal Shakespeare Company); *The Censor Or How to Put on A Political Play without Getting Arrested* (Central School of Speech and Drama); *Interference* (National Theatre of Scotland) and the critically acclaimed *Scenes from 68* Years* – shortlisted for the James Tait Black Award (Arcola Theatre). *Scenes* has also been mounted in San Francisco and in Tunisia in a British Council supported production under the new title *Trouf*. Further work includes *The Scar Test* (Soho Theatre) and *Plan D* (Tristan Bates Theatre, Meyer Whitworth Award nominee).

Hannah's online theatre work for young people includes an adaptation of *The Tempest* for Little Angel Puppet theatre and *Myths and Adventures from Ancient Greece* for Waterman Arts as well as *Mrs Scrooge* and *Not the Gingerbread Man* hosted by Fly High Stories online. She also adapted Ovid's *Penelope* as part of 15 Heroines at the Jermyn Street Theatre.

Hannah's radio plays include *The Unwelcome, Last of the Pearl Fishers* and *The Deportation Room* all for BBC Radio 4. Her first short film *The Record* took the Tommy Vine screenplay award and premiered at the Palestinian Film Festival in London in November 2019.

Hannah was the Bush Theatre London's writer on attachment in 2016/7 as part of Project 2036. Her awards include the Arab British Centre's Award for Culture in 2017 and the prestigious Heimbold Chairship for Villanova University, Philadelphia in 2021. She is a Resident Artist at Golden Thread, San Francisco and has been named a Creative Associate of the Samuel Beckett Archive, Reading University for 2021/22.

The Life of King Henry VIII: All is True

Or

Did My Heart Love til Now?

To my daughter and all her generation who I know will revisit the old stories, see them with fresh eyes and retell them in insightful ways. You are the future.

Characters

Queen Katharine
Princess Mary
King Henry VIII
Woman One
Woman Two
Gentleman
Buckingham
Norfolk
Cardinal Wolsey
Sergeant
Anne Bullen
Cromwell
Sands
Lovell
Chamberlain
Hope
Patience
Cardinal Campeius
Crier
The five women of The Visions
Surrey
Porter
Porter's woman
Elizabeth I (baby and adult)

Act One

Scene One

The court is all festivities and excitement. Singing, dancing, preparation. There is an anticipation. The king is due to return from France. We have a dance rehearsal – the audience are taught a section of the dance – everyone is getting ready. Then suddenly the trumpet sounds.

Queen Katharine *and* **Princess Mary** *enter the stage as* **King Henry** *enters through the yard.* **Mary** *is gently encouraged to the centre of the stage by her mother.* **King Henry** *and his retinue stand in the yard and watch as she sings Sonnet 116:*

Mary

Let me not to the marriage of true minds
Admit impediments. Love is not love
Which alters when it alteration finds,
Or bends with the remover to remove.
O no! it is an ever-fixed mark
That looks on tempests and is never shaken;
It is the star to every wand'ring bark,
Whose worth's unknown, although his height be taken.
Love's not Time's fool, though rosy lips and cheeks
Within his bending sickle's compass come;
Love alters not with his brief hours and weeks,
But bears it out even to the edge of doom.
If this be error and upon me prov'd,
I never writ, nor no man ever lov'd.

At the end **King Henry** *leaps on stage and swings his girl around.*

King Henry

Is she worth keeping? Why, she is a pearl
Whose price hath launch'd above a thousand ships
My Mary!
First and happiest hearers of the town
Our union with France is now complete.

A contract to celebrate, Let us all
go in together and drink a measure
and dance as is our pleasure – come!

The court cheers in approval as he embraces **Mary** *and his wife*
Katharine, *who has been looking proudly on all the while.*

Woman One
    The child has princely training, is manner'd as she is born.

Woman Two
    Would she were a Prince . . .

They watch the arriving dignitaries.

Woman One
    From Calais; and to England then;
    Where ne'er from France arriv'd more happy men.

The women regard the dignitaries.

Woman Two
    Is't possible the spells of France should juggle
    Men into such strange mysteries?

Woman One
    New customs,
    Though they be never so ridiculous,
    Nay, let 'em be unmanly, yet are follow'd.

Woman Two
    As far as I see, all the good our English
    Have got by the late voyage is but merely
    A fit or two o' the face.

Woman One
    Death! my lady,
    Their clothes are after such a pagan cut too,
    That, sure, they've worn out Christendom.

Noticing **Woman Two** *shivering.*

    Art cold?

Woman Two

My very lips might freeze to my teeth, my tongue to the roof
of my mouth, my heart in my belly, ere I should come by a
fire to
thaw me.

Woman One

I am cold myself.
O the fierce wretchedness that this French glory brings us!
O, who can hold a fire in his hand
By thinking on the frosty Caucasus?
Or cloy the hungry edge of appetite
By bare imagination of a feast?
Or wallow naked in December snow
By thinking on fantastic summer's heat?
O, no! the apprehension of the good
Gives but the greater feeling to the worse.
True is it that we have seen better days,

Woman Two

I think,
The peace between the French and us not values
The cost that did conclude it.

*They realise that the audience are listening to them and are annoyed
and embarrassed.*

Woman One

Remember where we are:
London, amongst a fickle wavering nation;
If they perceive dissension in our looks
And that within ourselves we disagree,
How will their grudging stomachs be provok'd
To wilful disobedience, and rebel!

Woman Two

Pray then –

Both Women

Let us go in together.

They exit.

Scene Two

London. An ante-chamber in the palace.

Enter **Norfolk** *at one door; at the other,* **Buckingham**.

Buckingham
Good morrow, and well met. How have ye done
Since last we saw in France?

Norfolk
I thank your grace,
Healthful; and ever since a fresh admirer
Of what I saw there.

Buckingham
An untimely ague
Stay'd me a prisoner in my chamber when
Those suns of glory, those two lights of men,
Met in the vale of Andren.

Norfolk
I was then present, saw them salute on horseback;
Beheld them, when they lighted, how they clung
In their embracement, as they grew together;

Buckingham
All the whole time
I was my chamber's prisoner.

Norfolk
Then you lost
The view of earthly glory: men might say,
Till this time pomp was single, but now married
To one above itself. Each following day
Became the next day's master, till the last
Made former wonders its. To-day the French,
All clinquant, all in gold, like heathen gods,
Shone down the English; and, to-morrow, they
Made Britain India: every man that stood
Show'd like a mine. All was royal.

Buckingham

All this was order'd by the good discretion
Of the right reverend Cardinal Wolsey
The devil speed him! no man's pie is freed
From his ambitious finger.

We watch the **Cardinal** *donning his finery in this next section.*

Norfolk

There's in him stuff that puts him to these ends;
For, being not propp'd by ancestry, whose grace
Chalks successors their way, nor call'd upon
For high feats done to the crown; neither allied
For eminent assistants; but, spider-like,
Out of his self-drawing web, he gives us note,
The force of his own merit makes his way
A gift that heaven gives for him, which buys
A place next to the king.

Buckingham

I cannot tell
What heaven hath given him, – let some graver eye
Pierce into that; but I can see his pride
Peep through each part of him: whence has he that,
If not from hell?
Why the devil,
Upon this French going out,
O, many
Have broke their backs with laying manors on 'em
For this great journey. What did this vanity
But minister communication of
A most poor issue?

Norfolk

Grievingly I think,
The peace between the French and us not values
The cost that did conclude it.
For France hath flaw'd the league, and hath attach'd
Our merchants' goods at Bourdeaux.

Buckingham

A proper title of a peace; and purchased
At a superfluous rate!
Why, all this business
Our reverend Cardinal Wolsey carried.

Norfolk

Like it your grace,
The state takes notice of the private difference
Betwixt you and the cardinal. I advise you –
And take it from a heart that wishes towards you
Honour and plenteous safety – that you read
The cardinal's malice and his potency
Together; to consider further that
What his high hatred would effect wants not
A minister in his power. You know his nature,
That he's revengeful, and I know his sword
Hath a sharp edge: it's long and, 't may be said,
It reaches far, and where 'twill not extend,
Thither he darts it.

Enter **Cardinal Wolsey** *to the yard, the purse borne before him, certain of the Guard, and two Secretaries with papers.* **Cardinal Wolsey** *in his passage fixeth his eye on* **Buckingham**, *and* **Buckingham** *on him, both full of disdain.*

Cardinal Wolsey

Our man in the Duke of Buckingham's house?

Chamberlain

Here!

Cardinal Wolsey

Where's his examination?

Cromwell

Here, so please you.

Cardinal Wolsey

Are you ready?

He hands him a purse.

Chamberlain
  Ay, please your grace.

Cardinal Wolsey
  Well, we shall then know more; and Buckingham
  Shall lessen this big look.

Cardinal Wolsey *and his train mount the stage and exit to the tiring house.*

Buckingham
  I read in's look
  Matter against me; and his eye reviled
  Me, as his abject object: at this instant
  He bores me with some trick: he's gone to the king;
  I'll follow and outstare him.

Norfolk
  Stay, my lord,
  And let your reason with your choler question
  What 'tis you go about: to climb steep hills
  Requires slow pace at first: anger is like
  A full-hot horse, who being allow'd his way,
  Self-mettle tires him. Not a man in England
  Can advise me like you: be to yourself
  As you would to your friend.

Buckingham
  I'll to the king;
  And from a mouth of honour quite cry down
  This Ipswich fellow's insolence; or proclaim
  There's difference in no persons.

Norfolk
  Be advised;
  Heat not a furnace for your foe so hot
  That it do singe yourself:

Buckingham
  Sir,
  I am thankful to you; and I'll go along

By your prescription: but this top-proud fellow,
I do know to be corrupt and treasonous.

Norfolk
Say not 'treasonous'.

Buckingham
To the king I'll say't; and make my vouch as strong
As shore of rock. Attend. This holy fox,
Or wolf, or both, – for he is equal ravenous
As he is subtle, and as prone to mischief
As able to perform't; his mind and place
Infecting one another, yea, reciprocally –
Only to show his pomp as well in France
As here at home, suggests the king our master
To this last costly treaty, the interview,
That swallow'd so much treasure, and like a glass
Did break i' the rinsing.

Norfolk
Faith, and so it did.

Buckingham
Let the king know,
As soon he shall by me, that thus the cardinal
Does buy and sell his honour as he pleases,
And for his own advantage.

Enter **Sergeant** *with two or three of the* **Guard**.

Sergeant
Sir,
My lord the Duke of Buckingham, and Earl
Of Hereford, Stafford, and Northampton, I
Arrest thee of high treason, in the name
Of our most sovereign king.

Buckingham
Lo, you, my lord,
The net has fall'n upon me! I shall perish
Under device and practise.

Sergeant
  'tis his highness' pleasure
  You shall to the Tower.

Buckingham
  My accuser is false; the o'er-great cardinal
  Hath show'd him gold; my life is spann'd already:
  I am the shadow of poor Buckingham,
  Whose figure even this instant cloud puts on,
  By darkening my clear sun. My lord, farewell.

Exit.

Scene Three

The same. The council-chamber.

Cornets. Enter **King Henry**, *his throne is pushed forward from the tiring house to centre stage and the doors closed behind him.*

Cardinal Wolsey *places himself under* **King Henry**'s *feet on his right side.* **Cromwell** *watches on from the side.*

Cardinal Wolsey (*to the* **King**)
  I do not like the office:
  But, sith I am enter'd in this cause so far,
  Prick'd to't by foolish honesty and love,
  I will go on.
  An army has he muster'd in his thoughts,
  Wherewith already my Lord is overrun.
  I do fear his period,
  To sheathe his knife in thee

King Henry (*to* **Wolsey**)
  My life itself, and the best heart of it,
  Thanks you for this great care: I stood i' the level
  Of a full-charged confederacy, and give thanks
  To you that choked it. Let be call'd before us
  That gentleman of Buckingham's; in person
  I'll hear him his confessions justify;

And point by point the treasons of his master
He shall again relate.

A noise within, crying 'Room for the Queen!' Enter **Queen
Katharine**, *ushered by* **Norfolk**, **Mary** *is hiding behind her
mother's skirts unseen by the* **King**, *she is shooed behind a pillar by
her mother's woman, Patience, where she sits, out of sight of the king,
listening to the rest of the scene. The* **Queen** *kneels.* **King Henry**
riseth from his state, takes her up, kisses and placeth her by him.

Queen Katharine
    Nay, we must longer kneel: I am a suitor.

King Henry
    Arise, and take place by us: half your suit
    Never name to us; you have half our power:
    The other moiety, ere you ask, is given;
    Repeat your will and take it.

Queen Katharine
    Thank your majesty.

King Henry
    Lady mine, proceed.

Queen Katharine
    I am solicited, not by a few,
    And those of true condition, that your subjects
    Are in great grievance: there have been commissions
    Sent down among 'em, which hath flaw'd the heart
    Of all their loyalties: wherein, although,
    My good lord cardinal, they vent reproaches
    Most bitterly on you, as putter on
    Of these exactions, yet the king our master –
    Whose honour heaven shield from soil! – even he
    escapes not
    Language unmannerly, yea, such which breaks
    The sides of loyalty, and almost appears
    In loud rebellion.

Norfolk
　Not almost appears,
　It doth appear; for, upon these taxations,
　The clothiers all, not able to maintain
　The many to them longing, have put off
　The spinsters, carders, fullers, weavers, who,
　Unfit for other life, compell'd by hunger
　And lack of other means, in desperate manner
　Daring the event to the teeth, are all in uproar,
　And danger serves among them!

King Henry
　Taxation!
　Wherein? and what taxation? My lord cardinal,
　You that are blamed for it alike with us,
　Know you of this taxation?

Cardinal Wolsey
　Please you, sir,
　I know but of a single part, in aught
　Pertains to the state; and front but in that file
　Where others tell steps with me.

Queen Katharine
　No, my lord,
　These exactions,
　Whereof my sovereign would have note,
　They say
　They are devised by you; or else you suffer
　Too hard an exclamation.

King Henry
　Still exaction!
　The nature of it? In what kind, let's know,
　Is this exaction?

Queen Katharine
　I am much too venturous
　In tempting of your patience; but am bolden'd
　Under your promised pardon. The subjects' grief

Comes through commissions, which compel from each
The sixth part of his substance, to be levied
Without delay; and the pretence for this
Is named, your union with France: this makes bold
mouths:
Tongues spit their duties out, and cold hearts freeze
Allegiance in them; their curses now
Live where their prayers did:
I would your highness
Would give it quick consideration, for
There is no primer business.

King Henry
By my life,
This is against our pleasure.

Cardinal Wolsey
And for me,
I have no further gone in this than by
A single voice; and that not pass'd me but
By learned approbation of the judges. If I am
Traduced by ignorant tongues, which neither know
My faculties nor person, yet will be
The chronicles of my doing, let me say
'Tis but the fate of place, and the rough brake
That virtue must go through. We must not stint
Our necessary actions, in the fear
To cope malicious censurers;
If we shall stand still,
In fear our motion will be mock'd or carp'd at,
We should take root here where we sit, or sit
State-statues only.

King Henry
Things done well,
And with a care, exempt themselves from fear;
Things done without example, in their issue
Are to be fear'd. Have you a precedent
Of this commission? I believe, not any.

We must not rend our subjects from our laws,
And stick them in our will. Sixth part of each?
A trembling contribution! Why, we take
From every tree lop, bark, and part o' the timber;
And, though we leave it with a root, thus hack'd,
The air will drink the sap. To every county
Where this is question'd send our letters, with
Free pardon to each man that has denied
The force of this commission: pray, look to't;
I put it to your care.

Cardinal Wolsey
A word with you.

To **Cromwell**.

Let there be letters writ to every shire,
Of the king's grace and pardon. The grieved commons
Hardly conceive of me; let it be noised
That through our intercession this revokement
And pardon comes: I shall anon advise you
Further in the proceeding.

Exit **Cromwell**.

Enter **Chamberlain**.

Queen Katharine
I am sorry that the Duke of Buckingham
Is run in your displeasure.

King Henry
It grieves many:
The gentleman is learn'd, and a most rare speaker;
To nature none more bound; his training such,
That he may furnish and instruct great teachers,
And never seek for aid out of himself. Yet see,
When these so noble benefits shall prove
Not well disposed, the mind growing once corrupt,
They turn to vicious forms, ten times more ugly
Than ever they were fair.

Sit by us; you shall hear –
This was his gentleman in trust – of him
Things to strike honour sad. Bid him recount
The fore-recited practices; whereof
We cannot feel too little, hear too much.

Cardinal Wolsey
Stand forth, and with bold spirit relate what you,
Most like a careful subject, have collected
Out of the Duke of Buckingham.

King Henry
Speak freely.

Chamberlain
First, it was usual with him, every day
It would infect his speech, that if the king
Should without male issue die, he'll carry it so
To make the sceptre his: these very words
I've heard him utter to his son-in-law,

We see **Mary** *pay attention to this. She looks upset, and listens all the more fervently from here.*

Mary *(aside)*
WITHOUT MALE ISSUE DIE?
Is not this female heir as well-deserving as a son?

Cardinal Wolsey
'*That if the king*
Should without male issue die'
Please your highness, note
This dangerous conception in this point.

Queen Katharine
My learn'd lord cardinal,
Deliver all with charity.

King Henry
Speak on:
How grounded he his title to the crown,
Upon our fail?

Queen Katharine (*to* **Chamberlain**)
  If I know you well,
  You were the duke's man, and lost your office
  On the complaint o' the tenants: take good heed
  You charge not in your spleen a noble person
  And spoil your nobler soul: I say, take heed;
  Yes, heartily beseech you.

King Henry
  Let him on.
  Go forward.

Chamberlain
  On my soul, I'll speak but truth.
  Being at Greenwich,
  After your highness had reproved the duke
  quoth he:
  'Why, I can smile, and murder whiles I smile,
  And cry 'Content' to that which grieves my heart,
  And wet my cheeks with artificial tears,
  And frame my face to all occasions.
  I can add colours to the chameleon,
  Change shapes with Proteus for advantages,
  And set the murderous Machiavel to school.
  Can I do this, and cannot get a crown?'

King Henry
  A giant traitor!

Cardinal Wolsey
  Now, madam, may his highness live in freedom,
  and this man out of prison?

Queen Katharine
  God mend all!

King Henry
  There's his period,
  To sheathe his knife in us. He is attach'd;
  Call him to present trial: if he may
  Find mercy in the law, 'tis his: if none,

Let him not seek 't of us: by day and night,
He's traitor to the height.

Exit all except **Mary**.

*Once they have all gone she comes out from her hiding. She wishes
she had not overheard all that she did. She addresses the audience.*

Mary
What I am, you right well know.
My father possesses the regal estate by right of
inheritance, which now by the same right descends unto
me. And to him always ye showed your selves most faithful
and loving subjects, and him obeyed and served as your
liege lord and king: and therefore I doubt not but you
will show your selves likewise to me his daughter.
I am the right and true inheritor to the crown of this
realm of England;
I am . . .
I am!

She storms off, furious at the idea her claim is not recognised.

Scene Four

A Hall in York Place.

Cardinal Wolsey *sits at a small table observing a longer table
around which are the guests, including* **Anne** *and divers other
Ladies and Gentlemen with* **Cromwell** *and the men,*
Chamberlain, **Sands**, *and* **Lovell** – *the men all drink and sing:*

Song – Cock in Hell

*My old chum Nick Nick Nick
He gets a kick kick kick
dressing to the right
dressing to the left
He likes to look smart
To eat his tasty tart*

But will he cum Nicky cum?
will he cum Nicky cum?

My old chum Nick Nick Nick
Walks with a stick stick stick
Down to the wood
Walk'll do him good
In the dark
With his tart
But will he cum Nicky cum?
will he cum Nicky cum?

But poor old Nick Nick Nick
Doesn't get a lick lick lick
Cos she sees his chap
Is havin a nap
So off she trots
As his fella rots
He won't cum Nicky cum
cum Nicky cum

My old mate Nick Nick Nick
He is so thick thick thick
He wants a date
But can't find a mate
So puts his pole
Into any old hole
But will he cum Nicky cum?
will he cum Nicky cum?

My old mate Nick Nick Nick
Is feeling sick sick sick
Not a cock in hell's chance
Of attracting a maid's glance
And so he droops
All the way to his boots
He won't cum Nicky cum

Not a cock in hell's chance to
cum Nicky cum.

The men gather round the women and are very over familiar and handsy. **Anne** *pushes off a man's attentions.*

Anne
O, that the gods
Would set me free from this unhallow'd place,
Though they did change me to the meanest bird
That flies i' the purer air!

Cromwell
The very thought of this fair company
Clapp'd wings to me.

Sands
Sir Thomas Lovell, had the cardinal
But half my lay thoughts in him, some of these
Should find a running banquet ere they rested,
I think would better please 'em: by my life,
They are a sweet society of fair ones.

Lovell
O, that your lordship were but now confessor
To one or two of these!

Sands
I would I were;
They should find easy penance.

Lovell
Faith, how easy?

Sands
As easy as a down-bed would afford it.

Chamberlain
Sweet ladies, will it please you sit? Sir Harry,
Place you that side; I'll take the charge of this:
His grace is entering. Nay, you must not freeze;
Two women placed together makes cold weather:
My Lord Sands, you are one will keep 'em waking;
Pray, sit between these ladies.

Sands

    By my faith,
    And thank your lordship. By your leave, sweet ladies:
    If I chance to talk a little wild, forgive me;
    I had it from my father.

Anne

    Was he mad, sir?

Sands

    O, very mad, exceeding mad, in love too:
    But he would bite none; just as I do now,
    He would kiss you twenty with a breath.

Kisses her.

Chamberlain

    Well said, my lord.

Anne *doesn't like* **Sands'** *attention and so moves away from him all the while admonishing herself.*

Anne

    Fie, fie! unknit that threatening unkind brow,
    Heed your lady's good advice at once Anne
    And dart not scornful glances from those eyes,
    It blots thy beauty as frosts do bite the meads,
    Confounds thy fame as whirlwinds shake fair buds,
    And in no sense is meet or amiable.
    A woman moved is like a fountain troubled,
    Muddy, ill-seeming, thick, bereft of beauty;
    And while it is so, none so dry or thirsty
    Will deign to sip or touch one drop of it.

Wolsey *has watched all this with interest, he stands and addresses the gathering.*

Cardinal Wolsey

    You're welcome, my fair guests: that noble lady,
    Or gentleman, that is not freely merry,
    Is not my friend: this, to confirm my welcome;
    And to you all, good health.

Drinks.

Sands
Your grace is noble:
Let me have such a bowl may hold my thanks,
And save me so much talking.

Cardinal Wolsey
My Lord Sands,
I am beholding to you: cheer your neighbours.
Ladies, you are not merry: gentlemen,
Whose fault is this?

Sands
The red wine first must rise
In their fair cheeks, my lord; then we shall have 'em
Talk us to silence.

Anne
You are a merry gamester,
My Lord Sands.

Sands
Yes, if I make my play.
Here's to your ladyship: and pledge it, madam,
For 'tis to such a thing, –

Anne
You cannot show me.

Sands
I told your grace they would talk anon.

Anne (*aside*)
I see a woman may be made a fool,
If she had not a spirit to resist.

Drum and trumpet.

Cardinal Wolsey
What's that?

Cromwell
Look out there, some of ye.

Exit **Chamberlain**.

Cardinal Wolsey
What warlike voice,
And to what end is this? Nay, ladies, fear not;
By all the laws of war you're privileged.

Re-enter **Chamberlain**.

Chamberlain
A noble troop of strangers;
For so they seem: they've left their barge and landed;
And hither make, as great ambassadors
From foreign princes.

Hautboys.

Enter **King Henry** *and others, as masquers, disguised.*

Ushered by the **Chamberlain**.

They pass directly before **Cardinal Wolsey**, *and gracefully
salute him.*

A noble company! What are their pleasures?

Chamberlain
Because they speak no English, thus they pray'd
To tell your grace, that, having heard by fame
Of this so noble and so fair assembly
This night to meet here, they could do no less
Out of the great respect they bear to beauty,
Crave leave to view these ladies and entreat
An hour of revels with 'em.

Cardinal Wolsey
Say, Lord Chamberlain,
They have done my poor house grace; for which I pay 'em
A thousand thanks, and pray 'em take their pleasures.

They choose Ladies for the dance.

King Henry *chooses* **Anne**.

Music.

King Henry *is mesmerised by* **Anne***. She's no fool, she knows this is the king and behaves appropriately, accommodatingly – more so than she had with the other men, yet if his hands stray too much she carefully puts them somewhere more appropriate.*

Dance and song.

> *O mistress mine, where are you roaming?*
> *O, stay and hear; your true love's coming,*
> *That can sing both high and low.*
> *Trip no further, pretty sweeting;*
> *Journeys end in lovers meeting,*
> *Every wise man's son doth know.*
> *What is love? 'Tis not hereafter;*
> *Present mirth hath present laughter;*
> *What's to come is still unsure.*
> *In delay there lies no plenty,*
> *Then come kiss me, sweet and twenty;*
> *Youth's a stuff will not endure.*

She is rebuffing the king's attention.

Anne
There is a fair behaviour in thee, my Lord;
And though that nature with a beauteous wall
Doth oft close in pollution, yet of thee
I will believe thou hast a mind that suits
With this thy fair and outward character.

King Henry
The fairest hand I ever touch'd! O beauty,
Till now I never knew thee!

Anne
My husband will know my beauty. And only he.

Cardinal Wolsey
My lord!

Chamberlain
Your grace?

Cardinal Wolsey
Pray, tell 'em thus much from me:
There should be one amongst 'em, by his person,
More worthy this place than myself; to whom,
If I but knew him, with my love and duty
I would surrender it.

Chamberlain
Such a one, they all confess,
There is indeed; which they would have your grace
Find out, and he will take it.

Cardinal Wolsey
Let me see, then.
By all your good leaves, gentlemen; here I'll make
My royal choice.

King Henry
Ye have found him, cardinal:

Unmasking.

You hold a fair assembly; you do well, lord.

Cardinal Wolsey
I am glad
Your grace is grown so pleasant.

King Henry
My Lord Chamberlain,
Prithee, come hither: what fair lady's that?

Chamberlain
An't please your grace, Sir Thomas Bullen's daughter –
The Viscount Rochford, – one of her highness' Queen
Katharine's women.

King Henry
By heaven, she is a dainty one. Sweetheart,
I were unmannerly, to take you out,
And not to kiss you.

Cardinal Wolsey
Your grace,
I fear, with dancing is a little heated.

King Henry
I fear, too much.

Cardinal Wolsey
There's fresher air, my lord,
In the next chamber.

He tries to steer **King Henry** *from* **Anne** *but the* **King** *takes her arm and leads her inside too.*

King Henry
Lead in your ladies, every one: sweet partner,
I must not yet forsake you: let's be merry:
Good my lord cardinal, I have half a dozen healths
To drink to these fair ladies, and a measure
To lead 'em once again; and then let's dream
Who's best in favour. Let the music knock it.

All have gone but **Wolsey**.

Cardinal Wolsey
Sir Thomas Bullen's Daughter. Anne?
Anne Bullen! No; I'll no Anne Bullens for him:
It shall be to the Duchess of Alencon,
The French king's sister: he shall marry her.

He exits determined to keep the **King** *and* **Anne** *apart.*

Reprise verse of Cock in Hell.

Act Two

Scene One

Westminster. A street.

Enter two Gentlewomen, meeting.

Woman One
Whither away so fast?

Woman Two
O, God save ye!
Even to the hall, to hear what shall become
Of the great Duke of Buckingham.

Woman One
I'll save you
That labour, madam. All's now done, but the ceremony
Of bringing back the prisoner.

Woman Two
Is he found guilty?

Woman One
Yes, truly is he, and condemn'd upon't.

Woman Two
I am sorry for't.

Woman One
So are a number more.

Woman Two
But, pray, how pass'd it?

Woman One
He pleaded still not guilty and alleged
Many sharp reasons to defeat the law.
The king's attorney on the contrary
Urged on the examinations, proofs, confessions
Of divers witnesses;

All these accused him strongly; which he fain
Would have flung from him, but, indeed, he could not:
And so his peers, upon this evidence,
Have found him guilty of high treason.

Woman Two
I do not think he fears death.

Woman One
Sure, he does not:
He never was so womanish; the cause
He may a little grieve at.

Woman Two
Certainly
The cardinal is the end of this.

Woman One
'Tis likely,
generally, whoever the king favours,
The cardinal instantly will find employment,
And far enough from court too.

Woman Two
All the commons
Hate him perniciously, and, o' my conscience,
Wish him ten fathom deep: this duke as much
They love and dote on; call him bounteous Buckingham,
The mirror of all courtesy;—

Woman One
Stay there, madam,
And see the noble ruin'd man you speak of.

Enter **Buckingham** *from his arraignment; tip-staves before him;*
the axe with the edge towards him; halberds on each side:
accompanied with **Lovell**, **Sands** *and common people.*

Woman Two
Let's stand close, and behold him.

Buckingham
All good people,
You that thus far have come to pity me,
Hear what I say, and then go home and lose me.
I have this day received a traitor's judgment,
And by that name must die: yet, heaven bear witness,
And if I have a conscience, let it sink me,
Even as the axe falls, if I be not faithful!
The law I bear no malice for my death;
'T has done, upon the premises, but justice:
But those that sought it I could wish more Christians:
Be what they will, I heartily forgive 'em:
You few that loved me,
And dare be bold to weep for Buckingham,
His noble friends and fellows, whom to leave
Is only bitter to him, only dying,
Go with me, like good angels, to my end;
And, as the long divorce of steel falls on me,
Make of your prayers one sweet sacrifice,
And lift my soul to heaven.

During the next speech **Buckingham** *is stripped of his worldy goods and clothes to signify his execution.*

Buckingham
When I came hither, I was Lord High Constable
And Duke of Buckingham; now, poor Edward Bohun:
Yet I am richer than my base accusers,
That never knew what truth meant: All good people,
Pray for me! I must now forsake ye: the last hour
Of my long weary life is come upon me. Farewell:
And when you would say something that is sad,
Speak how I fell. I have done; and God forgive me!

Exit **Buckingham.**

Woman One
It is full of pity
O God! that one might read the book of fate,
And see the revolution of the times

Make mountains level, and the continent,
Weary of solid firmness, melt itself
Into the sea;

Woman Two *is shocked at this revolutionary talk.*

Woman Two
Remember where we are:
London, amongst a fickle wavering nation.

Woman One
Mistake me not!
There is no living person that more detests, more stirs against,
Both in her private conscience and her place,
Defacers of a public peace, than I do.
But this is full of pity,
it calls,
I fear, too many curses on their heads
That were the authors.

Woman Two
If the duke be guiltless,
'Tis full of woe: yet I can give you inkling
Of an ensuing evil, if it fall,
Greater than this.

Woman One
Good angels keep it from us!
What may it be? You do not doubt my faith, lady?

Woman Two
This secret is so weighty, 'twill require
A strong faith to conceal it.

Woman One
Let me have it;
I do not talk much.

Woman Two
I am confident,
You shall, madam: did you not of late days hear

A buzzing of a separation
Between the king and Katharine?

Woman One

Yes, but it held not:
For when the king once heard it, out of anger
He sent command to the Lord Mayor straight
To stop the rumour, and allay those tongues
That durst disperse it.

Woman Two

But that slander, madam,
Is found a truth now: for it grows again
Fresher than e'er it was; and held for certain
The king will venture at it. Either the cardinal,
Or some about him near, have, out of malice
To the good queen, possess'd him with a scruple
That will undo her: to confirm this too,
Cardinal Campeius is arrived, from Rome;
As all think, for this business.

We see **Wolsey** *and* **Cromwell** *greet* **Campeius** *on stage – very friendly – and hand over a purse to him.*

Woman One

'Tis Cardinal Wolsey's doing.

Woman Two

I think you have hit the mark: but is't not cruel
That she should feel the smart of this? The cardinal
Will have his will, and she must fall.

They notice the audience listening.

Woman One

Remember where we are:

Woman Two

Pray then –

Both Women

Let us go in together.

Exit.

Scene Two

An ante-chamber in the palace.

Enter **Chamberlain**, **Norfolk** *and* **Surrey**.

Norfolk
Well met, my Lord Chamberlain.

Chamberlain
Good day to both your graces.

Surrey
How is the king employ'd?

Chamberlain
I left him private,
Full of sad thoughts and troubles.

Norfolk
What's the cause?

Chamberlain
It seems the marriage with his brother's wife
Has crept too near his conscience.

Surrey
No, his conscience
Has crept too near another lady.

Norfolk
'Tis so:
This is the cardinal's doing, the king-cardinal:
That blind priest, like the eldest son of fortune,
Turns what he list. The king will know him one day.

Surrey
Pray God he do! he'll never know himself else.

Norfolk
How holily he works in all his business!
And with what zeal! for, now
He dives into the king's soul, and there scatters
Dangers, doubts, wringing of the conscience,

Fears, and despairs; and all these for his marriage:
And out of all these to restore the king,
He counsels a divorce; a loss of her
That, like a jewel, has hung twenty years
About his neck, yet never lost her lustre;
Of her that loves him with that excellence
That angels love good men with; even of her
That, when the greatest stroke of fortune falls,
Will bless the king: and is not this course pious?

Chamberlain

Heaven keep me from such counsel! 'Tis most true
These news are every where; every tongue speaks 'em,
And every true heart weeps for't: all that dare
Look into these affairs see this main end,
The French king's sister. Heaven will one day open
The king's eyes, that so long have slept upon
This bold bad man Wolsey.

Surrey

Let's in;
And with some other business put the king
From these sad thoughts, that work too much upon him:
My lord, you'll bear us company?

Chamberlain

Excuse me;
The king has sent me otherwhere:
Health to your lordships.

Exit **Chamberlain***; and* **King Henry** *enters – he talks to himself and the audience.*

King Henry

I do affect the very ground, which is base, where her shoe, which is baser, guided by her foot, which is basest, doth tread. I shall be forsworn – which is a great argument of falsehood – if I love. And how can that be true love which is falsely attempted?
Love is a familiar; Love is a devil. There is no evil angel

but Love. Yet was Samson so tempted, and he had an
excellent strength; yet was Solomon so seduced, and he
had a very good wit.

Cupid's butt-shaft is too hard for Hercules' club, and
therefore too much odds for a Spaniard's rapier. The first
and second cause will not serve my turn; the passado he
respects not, the duello he regards not; his disgrace is to
be called boy, but his glory is to subdue men. Adieu,
valour; rust, rapier; be still, drum; for your manager is in
love; yea, he loveth. Assist me, some extemporal god of
rhyme, for I am sure I shall turn sonnet.

She has left me so unsatisfied,

And yet . . . I cannot have her unless we are wed . . .

Surrey

How sad he looks! sure, he is much afflicted.

King Henry

Who's there, ha?

Norfolk

Pray God he be not angry.

King Henry

Who's there, I say? How dare you thrust yourselves
Into my private meditations?
Who am I? ha?

Norfolk

A gracious king that pardons all offences
Malice ne'er meant: our breach of duty this way
Is business of estate; in which we come
To know your royal pleasure.

King Henry

Ye are too bold:
Go to; I'll make ye know your times of business:
Is this an hour for temporal affairs, ha?

Enter **Cardinal Wolsey** *and* **Cardinal Campeius**, *with a
commission.*

Who's there? My good lord cardinal? O my Wolsey,
The quiet of my wounded conscience;
Thou art a cure fit for a king.

To **Cardinal Campeius**.

You're welcome,
Most learned reverend sir, into our kingdom:
Use us and it.

To **Cardinal Wolsey**.

My good lord, have great care
I be not found a talker.

Cardinal Wolsey
Sir, you cannot.
I would your grace would give us but an hour
Of private conference.

King Henry (*To* **Norfolk** *and* **Surrey**)
We are busy; go.

Norfolk *and* **Surrey** *share a knowing and concerned look
then exit.*

Cardinal Wolsey
Your grace has given a precedent of wisdom
Above all princes, in committing freely
Your scruple to the voice of Christendom:
Who can be angry now? What envy reach you?
Rome, the nurse of judgment,
Invited by your noble self, hath sent
One general tongue unto us, this good man,
This just and learned priest, Cardinal Campeius;
Whom once more I present unto your highness.

King Henry
And once more in mine arms I bid him welcome,
And thank the holy conclave for their loves:
They have sent me such a man I would have wish'd for.

Cardinal Campeius

Your grace must needs deserve all strangers' loves,
You are so noble. To your highness' hand
I tender my commission; by whose virtue,
The court of Rome commanding, you, my lord
Cardinal of York, are join'd with me their servant
In the unpartial judging of this business.

King Henry

Two equal men. The queen shall be acquainted
Forthwith for what you come.

Cardinal Wolsey

I know your majesty has always loved her
So dear in heart, not to deny her that
A woman of less place might ask by law:
Scholars allow'd freely to argue for her.

King Henry

Ay, and the best she shall have; and my favour
To him that does best: God forbid else.
Things done well, and with a care, exempt themselves
from fear:
Things done without example, in their issue
Are to be fear'd.

He is vacillating.

Cardinal Wolsey

Remember Leviticus 20 my Lord
'The man that taketh his brother's wife, committeth
filthines, because he hath uncovered his brother's shame:
they shall be childless.'

King Henry (*aside*)

All that lives must die, Passing through nature to eternity.
But to die without issue . . .
When beggars die, there are no comets seen; The heavens
themselves blaze forth the death of princes.
But to die without issue . . .
'Tis a vile thing to die, When men are unprepared and

look not for it . . .
But to die without a son!
Impossible.

He is resolved.

(Aloud.)
The most convenient place that I can think of
For the good queen's tribunal is Black-Friars;
There ye shall meet about this weighty business.
My Wolsey, see it furnish'd. O, my lord,
Would it not grieve an able man to leave
So sweet a bedfellow? But, conscience, conscience!
O, 'tis a tender place; and I must leave her.

They exit.

Scene Three

An ante-chamber of the Queen's apartments.

Enter **Anne** *and* **Hope**.

Anne *is wearing French-style garments and* **Hope** *removes them, replacing them for the more English fashion –* **Anne** *is reluctant. Throughout the scene as they discuss their sadness at* **Queen Katharine**'s *fall we have the irony that* **Anne** *is being made up to delight the* **King**.

Hope
Do you hear me madam?
I say, the talk is all of France
'Their clothes are after such a pagan cut too,
That, sure, they've worn out Christendom'
Quoth she. Allez. Off.

She is removing something and catches **Anne** *with a pin on her neck.* **Anne** *says 'OUCH!' holding her neck.*

Hope
Are you hurt?

Anne

Not for that neither: here's the pang that pinches:
His Highness having lived so long with her, and she
So good a lady that no tongue could ever
Pronounce dishonour of her; by my life,
She never knew harm-doing: O, now, after
So many courses of the sun enthroned,
Still growing in a majesty and pomp, the which
To leave a thousand-fold more bitter than
'Tis sweet at first to acquire, – after this process,
To give her the avaunt! It is a pity
Would move a monster.

Hope

Hearts of most hard temper
Melt and lament for her.

Anne

O, God's will! much better
She ne'er had known pomp: though't be temporal,
Yet, if that quarrel, fortune, do divorce
It from the bearer, 'tis a sufferance panging
As soul and body's severing.

Hope

Alas, poor lady!
She's a stranger now again.

Anne

So much the more
Must pity drop upon her. Verily,
I swear, 'tis better to be lowly born,
And range with humble livers in content,
Than to be perk'd up in a glistering grief,
And wear a golden sorrow.

Hope

Our content
Is our best having.

Anne

To be a Queen, and wear a Crown, is a thing more
glorious to them that see it, than it is pleasant to them that
bear it
By my troth and maidenhead,
I would not be a queen.

Hope

Beshrew me, I would,
And venture maidenhead for't; and so would you,
For all this spice of your hypocrisy:
You, that have so fair parts of woman on you,
Have too a woman's heart; which ever yet
Affected eminence, wealth, sovereignty;
Which, to say sooth, are blessings; and which gifts,
Saving your mincing, the capacity
Of your soft cheveril conscience would receive,
If you might please to stretch it.

Anne

Nay, good troth.

Hope

Yes, troth, and troth; you would not be a queen?

Anne

No, not for all the riches under heaven.

Hope

'Tis strange: a three-pence bow'd would hire me,
Old as I am, to queen it: but, I pray you,
What think you of a duchess? have you limbs
To bear that load of title?

Anne

No, in truth.

Hope

Then you are weakly made: pluck off a little;
I would not be a young count in your way,
For more than blushing comes to: if your back

Cannot vouchsafe this burthen,'tis too weak
Ever to get a boy.

Anne

How you do talk!
I swear again, I would not be a queen
For all the world.

Hope

The lady doth protest too much, methinks.
In faith, for little England
You'd venture an emballing: I myself
Would for Carnarvonshire, although there long'd
No more to the crown but that. – Lo, who comes here?

Enter **Chamberlain**.

Chamberlain

Good morrow, ladies. What were't worth to know
The secret of your conference?

Anne

My good lord,
Not your demand; it values not your asking:
Our mistress' Queen Katharine's sorrows we were pitying.

Chamberlain

It was a gentle business, and becoming
The action of good women: there is hope
All will be well.

Anne

Now, I pray God, amen!

Chamberlain

You bear a gentle mind, and heavenly blessings
Follow such creatures. That you may, fair lady,
Perceive I speak sincerely, and high note's
Ta'en of your many virtues, the king's majesty
Commends his good opinion of you, and
Does purpose honour to you no less flowing
Than Marchioness of Pembroke: to which title

A thousand pound a year, annual support,
Out of his grace he adds.

Anne
I do not know
What kind of my obedience I should tender;
More than my all is nothing: nor my prayers
Are not words duly hallow'd, nor my wishes
More worth than empty vanities; yet prayers and wishes
Are all I can return. Beseech your lordship,
Vouchsafe to speak my thanks and my obedience,
As from a blushing handmaid, to his highness;
Whose health and royalty I pray for.

Chamberlain
Lady,
I shall not fail to approve the fair conceit
The king hath of you.

Aside.

I have perused her well;
Beauty and honour in her are so mingled
That they have caught the king: and who knows yet
But from this lady may proceed a gem
To lighten all this isle?

To **Anne**.

I'll to the king,
And say I spoke with you.

Anne
My honour'd lord.

Exit **Chamberlain**.

Hope
Why, this it is; see, see!
I have been begging sixteen years in court,
Am yet a courtier beggarly, nor could
Come pat betwixt too early and too late

For any suit of pounds; and you, O fate!
A very fresh-fish here – fie, fie, fie upon
This compell'd fortune! – have your mouth fill'd up
Before you open it.

Anne

This is strange to me.

Hope

There was a lady once, 'tis an old story,
That would not be a queen, that would she not,
For all the mud in Egypt: have you heard it?

Anne

Come, you are pleasant.

Hope

With your theme, I could
O'ermount the lark. The Marchioness of Pembroke!
A thousand pounds a year for pure respect!
No other obligation! By my life,
That promises moe thousands: honour's train
Is longer than his foreskirt. By this time
I know your back will bear a duchess: say,
Are you not stronger than you were?

Anne

Good lady,
Make yourself mirth with your particular fancy,
And leave me out on't. Would I had no being,
If this salute my blood a jot: it faints me,
To think what follows.
The queen is comfortless, and we forgetful
In our long absence: pray, do not deliver
What here you've heard to her.

Hope

What do you think me?

Exit **Hope**.

Anne

    I do think it is their husbands' faults
    If wives do fall: say that they slack their duties,
    And pour our treasures into foreign laps,
    Or else break out in peevish jealousies.
    But, love me? Why, it must be requited.
    What is a woman,
    If her chief good and market of her time
    Be but to sleep and feed? A beast, no more.
    Sure he that made us with such large discourse,
    Looking before and after, gave us not
    That capability and godlike reason
    To fust in us unus'd.
    The king must be requited therefore while
    I live to say 'This thing's to do,'
    Sith I have cause, and will, and strength, and means
    To do't. Therefore I shall. Marry I shall.

Scene Four

Trumpets, sennet and cornets.

*Music here should be the tune from the opening song (**Mary**) but arranged in a formal stately instrumental.*

King Henry *enters and takes place under the cloth of state;* **Cardinal Wolsey** *and* **Cardinal Campeius** *sit under him as judges.* **Cromwell** *watches on.*

Queen Katharine *enters with* **Patience** *and takes a place some distance from* **King Henry**.

Among the court is also **Surrey**.

We see **Mary** *watching from the Musicians' gallery as everyone takes their places, she is spotted by* **Patience**, *who signals for an attendant to take her out – she doesn't want her watching.* **Mary** *reluctantly allows herself to be led away.*

Cardinal Wolsey

Whilst our commission from Rome is read,
Let silence be commanded.

King Henry

What's the need?
It hath already publicly been read,
We seek to discover if our marriage be lawful or no,
And on all sides the authority allow'd;
You may, then, spare that time.

Queen Katharine *rises out of her chair, agitated, goes to* **King Henry** *and kneels at his feet. She's desperate and behaving in a way that is unlike her – she wants to appeal, to be heard – by her husband, the man, not the king.*

Queen Katharine

Alas, sir,
In what have I offended you? what cause
Hath my behaviour given to your displeasure,
That thus you should proceed to put me off,
And take your good grace from me?
I, Beyond all limit of what else i' th' world,
Do love, prize, honour you: Love you my Lord.

No reaction to this from the **King**, **Queen Katharine** *is getting more desperate.*

Heaven witness,
I have been to you a true and humble wife,
At all times to your will conformable;
Ever in fear to kindle your dislike,
Yea, subject to your countenance, glad or sorry
As I saw it inclined: when was the hour
I ever contradicted your desire,
Or made it not mine too? Or which of your friends
Have I not strove to love, although I knew
He were mine enemy? what friend of mine
That had to him derived your anger, did I
Continue in my liking? nay, gave notice

He was from thence discharged. Sir, call to mind
That I have been your wife, in this obedience,
Upward of twenty years, and have been blest
With many children by you

*The **King** looks at her sharply.*

– though they are lost
Grief fills the room up of my absent children,
Lies in their beds, walks up and down with me,
Yet there is your Pearl, your Mary.

King Henry *looks down or away, he cannot meet her gaze.*

If, in the course
And process of this time, you can report,
And prove it too, against mine honour aught,
My bond to wedlock, or my love and duty,
Against your sacred person, in God's name,
Turn me away; and let the foul'st contempt
Shut door upon me, and so give me up
To the sharp'st kind of justice.

*She is getting nothing from the **King** so takes a deep breath, steeling
herself – gathering up all her strength and grace she attacks the rest
of the proceedings as a true queen. Formal and clear.*

Please you sir,
The king, your father, was reputed for
A prince most prudent, of an excellent
And unmatch'd wit and judgment: Ferdinand,
My father, king of Spain, was reckon'd one
The wisest prince that there had reign'd by many
A year before: it is not to be question'd
That they had gather'd a wise council to them
Of every realm, that did debate this business,
Who deem'd our marriage lawful: wherefore I humbly
Beseech you, sir, to spare me, till I may
Be by my friends in Spain advised; whose counsel
I will implore: if not, i' the name of God,
Your pleasure be fulfill'd!

Mary *sneaks back in and watches from the Musicians' gallery – we see her though the* **King** *and* **Queen** *do not.*

Cardinal Wolsey
You have here, lady,
And of your choice, these reverend fathers; men
Of singular integrity and learning,
Yea, the elect o' the land, who are assembled
To plead your cause: it shall be therefore bootless
That longer you desire the court; as well
For your own quiet, as to rectify
What is unsettled in the king.

Cardinal Campeius
His grace
Hath spoken well and justly: therefore, madam,
It's fit this royal session do proceed;
And that, without delay, their arguments
Be now produced and heard.

Queen Katharine
Lord cardinal,
To you I speak.

Cardinal Wolsey
Be patient yet.

Queen Katharine
I will, when you are humble; nay, before,
Or God will punish me. I do believe,
Induced by potent circumstances, that
You are mine enemy, and make my challenge
You shall not be my judge: for it is you
Have blown this coal betwixt my lord and me;
Which God's dew quench! Therefore I say again,
I utterly abhor, yea, from my soul
Refuse you for my judge; whom, yet once more,
I hold my most malicious foe, and think not
At all a friend to truth.

Cardinal Wolsey
    I do profess
    You speak not like yourself; who ever yet
    Have stood to charity, and display'd the effects
    Of disposition gentle, and of wisdom
    O'ertopping woman's power. Madam, you do me wrong:
    I have no spleen against you; nor injustice
    For you or any: how far I have proceeded,
    Or how far further shall, is warranted
    By a commission from the consistory,
    Yea, the whole consistory of Rome. You charge me
    That I have blown this coal: I do deny it:
    The king is present: if it be known to him
    That I gainsay my deed, how may he wound,
    And worthily, my falsehood! yea, as much
    As you have done my truth. If he know
    That I am free of your report, he knows
    I am not of your wrong. Therefore in him
    It lies to cure me: and the cure is, to
    Remove these thoughts from you: the which before
    His highness shall speak in, I do beseech
    You, gracious madam, to unthink your speaking
    And to say so no more.

Queen Katharine
    My lord, my lord,
    I am a simple woman, much too weak
    To oppose your cunning. You're meek and
    humble-mouth'd;
    You sign your place and calling, in full seeming,
    With meekness and humility; but your heart
    Is cramm'd with arrogancy, spleen, and pride.
    You have, by fortune and his highness' favours,
    Gone slightly o'er low steps and now are mounted
    Where powers are your retainers, and your words,
    Domestics to you, serve your will as't please
    Yourself pronounce their office. I must tell you,
    You tender more your person's honour than

Your high profession spiritual: that again
I do refuse you for my judge; and here,
Before you all, appeal unto the Pope,
To bring my whole cause 'fore his holiness,
And to be judged by him.

She curtsies to **King Henry**, *and leaves.*

Cardinal Campeius
The queen is obstinate,
Stubborn to justice, apt to accuse it, and
Disdainful to be tried by't: 'tis not well.
She's going away.

Cardinal Wolsey
Call her again.

Crier
Katharine Queen of England, come into the court.

Patience
Madam, you are call'd back.

Queen Katharine
They vex me past my patience! Pray you, pass on:
I will not tarry; no, nor ever more
Upon this business my appearance make
In any of their courts.

Exit **Queen Katharine** *with* **Patience** *and her Attendants.*

King Henry *is impressed by her strength of will.*

King Henry
Go thy ways, Kate:
That man i' the world who shall report he has
A better wife, let him in nought be trusted,
For speaking false in that.

Cardinal Wolsey
Most gracious sir,
In humblest manner I require your highness,
That it shall please you to declare, in hearing

Of all these ears
whether ever I
Did broach this business to your highness; or
Laid any scruple in your way, which might
Induce you to the question on't?

King Henry
My lord cardinal,
I do excuse you; yea, upon mine honour,
I free you from't.
Now, what moved me to't,
I will be bold with time and your attention:

Mary *is listening hard.*

Then mark the inducement. Thus it came; give heed to't:
My conscience first received a tenderness,
Scruple, and prick, on certain speeches utter'd
By the Bishop of Bayonne, then French ambassador;
Who had been hither sent on the debating
A marriage 'twixt the Duke of Orleans and
Our daughter Mary: i' the progress of this business,
Ere a determinate resolution, he did require a respite;
Whether our daughter were legitimate.

Mary *reacts to this.*

Respecting this our marriage with the dowager,
Sometimes our brother's wife. This respite shook
The bosom of my conscience. First, methought
I stood not in the smile of heaven; that my lady's womb,
If it conceived a male child by me, should
Do no more offices of life to't than
The grave does to the dead; for her male issue
Or died where they were made, or shortly after
This world had air'd them: hence I took a thought,
This was a judgment on me; that my kingdom,
Well worthy the best heir o' the world, should not
Be gladded in't by me: then follows, that
I weigh'd the danger which my realms stood in

By this my issue's fail; and that gave to me
Many a groaning throe. Thus hulling in
The wild sea of my conscience, I did steer
Toward this remedy, whereupon we are
Now present here together: that's to say,
I meant to rectify my conscience, –
For no dislike i' the world against the person
Of the good queen.

Cardinal Campeius
So please your highness,
The queen being absent, 'tis a needful fitness
That we adjourn this court till further day:
Meanwhile must be an earnest motion
Made to the queen, to call back her appeal
She intends unto his holiness.

King Henry (*aside*)
I may perceive
This church trifles with me: I abhor
This dilatory sloth and tricks of Rome.
Ambitious churchmen, if thou cannot help me,
leave me now
Or I needs must
Break up the church . . .
I must

(*Aloud.*)
Break up the court:
I say, set on.

Exit in manner as they entered.

But not before **Surrey** *approaches* **King Henry** *and gives him*
Wolsey*'s letters surreptitiously,*

Surrey
My lord these letters have fallen in my path.

He continues speaking quietly to the **King** *as they exit.*

Mary

    Scarce can I speak, my choler is so great.
    O, I could hew up rocks and fight with flint,
    I am so angry at these abject terms;
    And now, like Ajax Telamonius,
    On sheep or oxen could I spend my fury.
    I am more like a king, more kingly in my thoughts;
    But I must make fair weather yet awhile,
    Till I be grown and more strong.
    But then – then I will have such revenges
    That all the world shall – I will do such things –
    What they are yet, I know not; but they shall be
    The terrors of the earth! You think I'll weep.
    No, I'll not weep.

She exits – she does not weep.

Act Three

Scene One

Queen Katharine *and her Women are in their rooms.*

Queen Katharine
Take thy lute, wench: my soul grows sad with troubles;
play, and disperse 'em, if thou canst: leave working.
My thoughts are whirled like a potter's wheel;
I know not where I am nor what I do.

Music plays.

Enter **Patience**.

Queen Katharine
How now!

Patience
An't please your grace, the two great cardinals
Wait in the presence.

Queen Katharine
Pray their graces
To come near.

Exit **Patience**.

What can be their business
With me, a poor weak woman, fall'n from favour?
I do not like their coming. Now I think on't,
They should be good men; their affairs as righteous:
But all hoods make not monks.

Enter **Cardinal Wolsey** *and* **Cardinal Campeius**.

Cardinal Wolsey
Peace to your highness!

Queen Katharine
Your graces find me here part of a housewife,
I would be all, against the worst may happen.
What are your pleasures with me, reverend lords?

Cardinal Wolsey

May it please you noble madam, to withdraw
Into your private chamber, we shall give you
The full cause of our coming.

Queen Katharine

Speak it here:
There's nothing I have done yet, o' my conscience,
Deserves a corner: would all other women
Could speak this with as free a soul as I do!
My lords, I care not, so much I am happy
Above a number, if my actions
Were tried by every tongue, every eye saw 'em,
Envy and base opinion set against 'em,
I know my life so even. If your business
Seek me out, and that way I am wife in,
Out with it boldly: truth loves open dealing.

Cardinal Wolsey

Noble lady,
I am sorry my integrity should breed,
And service to his majesty and you,
So deep suspicion, where all faith was meant.
We come not by the way of accusation,
To taint that honour every good tongue blesses,
Nor to betray you any way to sorrow,
You have too much, good lady; but to know
How you stand minded in the weighty difference
Between the king and you;

Cardinal Campeius

Most honour'd madam,
My Lord of York,
Offers, as I do, in a sign of peace,
His service and his counsel.

Queen Katharine (*aside*)

To betray me. –
My lords, I thank you both for your good wills;
Ye speak like honest men; pray God, ye prove so!

But how to make ye suddenly an answer,
In such a point of weight, so near mine honour, –
More near my life, I fear, – with my weak wit,
And to such men of gravity and learning,
In truth, I know not
good your graces,
Let me have time and counsel for my cause:
Alas, I am a woman, friendless, hopeless!

Cardinal Wolsey
Madam, you wrong the king's love with these fears:

Queen Katharine
His love?

Cardinal Wolsey
Your hopes and friends are infinite.

Queen Katharine
But little for my profit: can you think, lords,
That any Englishman dare give me counsel?
Or be a known friend, 'gainst his highness' pleasure,
Though he be grown so desperate to be honest,
And live a subject? Nay, forsooth, my friends,
They that must weigh out my afflictions,
They that my trust must grow to, live not here:
They are, as all my other comforts, far hence
In mine own country, lords.

Cardinal Campeius
I would your grace
Would leave your griefs, and take my counsel.

Queen Katharine
How, sir?

Cardinal Campeius
Put your main cause into the king's protection;
He's loving and most gracious: 'twill be much
Both for your honour better and your cause;
For if the trial of the law o'ertake ye,
You'll part away disgraced.

Cardinal Wolsey
  He tells you rightly.

Queen Katharine
  Ye tell me what ye wish for both, – my ruin:
  Is this your Christian counsel? out upon ye!
  Heaven is above all yet; there sits a judge
  That no king can corrupt.

Cardinal Campeius
  Your rage mistakes us.

Queen Katharine
  The more shame for ye: holy men I thought ye,
  Upon my soul, two reverend cardinal virtues;
  But cardinal sins and hollow hearts I fear ye:
  Mend 'em, for shame, my lords. Is this your comfort?

Cardinal Wolsey
  Madam, this is a mere distraction;
  You turn the good we offer into envy.

Queen Katharine
  Ye turn me into nothing: woe upon ye
  And all such false professors! Would you have me –
  If you have any justice, any pity;
  If ye be any thing but churchmen's habits –
  Put my sick cause into his hands that hates me?
  For him I would walk barefoot to Palestine
  Alas, has banish'd me his bed already,
  His love, too long ago! I am old, my lords,
  And all the fellowship I hold now with him
  Is only my obedience. What can happen
  To me above this wretchedness?

Cardinal Campeius
  Your fears are worse.

Queen Katharine
  Have I lived thus long – let me speak myself,
  Since virtue finds no friends – a wife, a true one?

A woman, I dare say without vain-glory,
Never yet branded with suspicion?
Have I with all my full affections
Still met the king? loved him next heaven?
Obey'd him?
Been, out of fondness, superstitious to him?
Almost forgot my prayers to content him?
And am I thus rewarded? 'tis not well, lords.

Cardinal Wolsey

Madam, you wander from the good we aim at.
If your grace
Could but be brought to know our ends are honest,
You'ld feel more comfort: why should we, good lady,
Upon what cause, wrong you? Alas, our places,
The way of our profession is against it:
We are to cure such sorrows, not to sow 'em.

Queen Katharine

My lord, I dare not make myself so guilty,
To give up willingly that noble title
Your master wed me to: nothing but death
Shall e'er divorce my dignities.

Cardinal Wolsey

For goodness' sake, consider what you do;
How you may hurt yourself, ay, utterly
Grow from the king's acquaintance, by this carriage.
The hearts of princes kiss obedience,
So much they love it; but to stubborn spirits
They swell, and grow as terrible as storms.
I know you have a gentle, noble temper,
A soul as even as a calm: pray, think us
Those we profess, peace-makers, friends, and servants.

Cardinal Campeius

If you please
To trust us in your business, we are ready
To use our utmost studies in your service.

Queen Katharine (*aside*)
  Annulment or the long divorce of steel.

(*Aloud.*)
  Do what ye will, my lords: and, pray, forgive me,
  If I have used myself unmannerly;
  You know I am a woman, lacking wit
  To make a seemly answer to such persons.
  Pray, do my service to his majesty:
  He has my heart yet; and shall have my prayers
  While I shall have my life.

The **Cardinals** *bow and exit.* **Queen Katharine** *is in turmoil.*

  Ye turn me into nothing:
  Ye would turn me into nothing:
  Men should be what they seem;
  Or those that be not, would they might seem none!
  Trust not him that hath once broken faith.

The **King** *and* **Anne** *appear dancing to the following song and kissing in the Musicians' gallery. They have just been married.*

Song

The five women who we see in the Vision later in the play – who represent **King Henry**'s *future wives – sing:*

  *He will steal, sir, an egg out of a cloister; for rapes
  and ravishments he parallels Nessus. He professes not keeping of
  oaths; in breaking 'em he is stronger than Hercules. He will lie,
  sir, with such volubility that you would think truth were a fool.
  Drunkenness is his best virtue, for he will be swine-drunk; and
  in his sleep he does little harm, save to his bedclothes about
  him; but they know his conditions and lay him in straw. I have
  but little more to say, sir, of his honesty. He has everything
  that an honest man should not have; what an honest man should
  have he has nothing.*

Interval.

Scene Two

A reprise of the honest man song from the end of the first half.

Ante-chamber to King Henry's apartment.

King *enters – he has the letters* **Surrey** *gave him. He reads.*

The gentlewomen watch on.

Woman One
But soft! Soft! Here comes the king.
Sure, he is much afflicted.

Woman Two
He has letters un'sealed.

Woman One
The same given him by my lord of Surrey – what's within?

Woman Two
All torment, trouble, wonder and amazement
Inhabits here.

The women watch on until he has revealed the letters' contents then exit.

King Henry
What piles of wealth hath Wolsey accumulated
To his own portion! and what expense by the hour
Seems to flow from him! How, i' the name of thrift,
Does he rake this together!
It may well be;
There is a mutiny in's mind.
And what's here?

(Reading.)
'Stay your judgment o' the divorce; for if
It take place, I do perceive
My king is tangled in affection to
A creature of the queen's, Lady Anne Bullen.'
A creature of the queen's?

HA!

Now, sir, you speak of one
The most remark'd i' the kingdom. My wife.
Tis too late Wolsey we are already wed.
Love and meekness, lord,
Become a churchman better than ambition:
To my face you play the spaniel,
And think with wagging of your tongue to win me;
But here is the truth
Thou hast a cruel nature and a bloody.
Men should be what they seem;
Or those that be not, would they might seem none!
Trust not him that hath once broken faith.
Ye blew the fire that burns ye Wolsey: now have at ye.

He exits, continuing to read.

Enter **Norfolk, Surrey,** *and* **Chamberlain.**

Chamberlain

My lords, you speak your pleasures:
What he deserves of you and me I know;
What we can do to him, though now the time
Gives way to us, I much fear. If you cannot
Bar his access to the king, never attempt
Any thing on him; for he hath a witchcraft
Over the king in's tongue.

Norfolk

O, fear him not;
His spell in that is out: the king hath found
Matter against him that for ever mars
The honey of his language. No, he's settled,
Not to come off, in his displeasure.

Chamberlain

Sir,
I should be glad to hear such news as this
Once every hour.

Norfolk
Believe it, this is true:
In the divorce his contrary proceedings
Are all unfolded.

Chamberlain
How came
His practices to light?

Surrey
Most strangely.
The cardinal's letters to the Pope miscarried.

Norfolk
Aye 'miscarried'.

Surrey
And came to the eye o' the king: wherein was read,
How that the cardinal did entreat his holiness
To stay the judgment o' the divorce; for if
It did take place, 'I do,' quoth he, 'perceive
My king is tangled in affection to
A creature of the queen's, Lady Anne Bullen.'

Chamberlain
Has the king this?

Norfolk
Believe it.
The king in this perceives him, how he coasts
And hedges his own way. But in this point
All his tricks founder, and he brings his physic
After his patient's death: the king already
Hath married the fair lady.

Surrey
Now, all my joy
Trace the conjunction!

Chamberlain
My amen to't!

Norfolk
  All men's!
  There's order given for her coronation:
  Marry, this is yet but young, and may be left
  To some ears unrecounted. But, my lords,
  She is a gallant creature, and complete
  In mind and feature: I persuade me, from her
  Will fall some blessing to this land,
  A gem to lighten this isle.

Chamberlain
  But, will the king
  Digest this letter of the cardinal's?

Surrey
  There be moe wasps that buzz about his nose
  Will make this sting the sooner. Cardinal Campeius
  Is stol'n away to Rome; hath ta'en no leave;
  Has left the cause o' the king unhandled; and
  Is posted, as the agent of our cardinal,
  To second all his plot. I do assure you
  The king cried Ha! at this.

Chamberlain
  Now, God incense him,
  And let him cry Ha! louder!

Surrey
  Shortly, I believe,
  His second marriage shall be publish'd, and
  Her coronation. Katharine no more
  Shall be call'd queen, but princess dowager
  And widow to Prince Arthur.

Enter **Cardinal Wolsey**, *the men move so he cannot see them and observe him, he is agitated.*

Wolsey (*aside*)
  It shall be to the Duchess of Alencon,
  I say again the Duchess of Alencon,
  The French king's sister: he shall marry her.

Anne Bullen! No; I'll no Anne Bullens for him:
There's more in't than fair visage. Bullen!
No, we'll no Bullens. Speedily I wish
To hear from Rome. The Marchioness of Pembroke!
The late queen's gentlewoman,
a knight's daughter,
To be her mistress' mistress! the queen's queen!
This candle burns not clear: 'tis I must snuff it;
Then out it goes. What though I know her virtuous
And well deserving? yet I know her for
A spleeny Lutheran with no love for the forgotten church
in Rome; and not wholesome to
Our cause that she should lie i' the bosom of
Our hard-ruled king.

Enter **King Henry**, *who takes his seat.*

Cardinal Wolsey

Ever God bless your highness!

King Henry

Good my lord,
You are full of heavenly stuff,
you have scarce time
To steal from spiritual leisure a brief span
To keep your earthly audit: sure, in that
I deem you an ill husband, and am glad
To have you therein my companion.

Cardinal Wolsey

Sir,
For holy offices I have a time; a time
To think upon the part of business which
I bear i' the state; and nature does require
Her times of preservation, which perforce
I, her frail son, amongst my brethren mortal,
Must give my tendence to.

King Henry

You have said well.

And 'tis a kind of good deed to say well:
And yet words are no deeds.

Cardinal Wolsey (*aside*)
What should this mean?

King Henry
Have I not made you,
The prime man of the state? I pray you, tell me,
If what I now pronounce you have found true:
And, if you may confess it, say withal,
If you are bound to us or no. What say you?

Cardinal Wolsey
My sovereign, I confess your royal graces,
Shower'd on me daily, have been more than could
My studied purposes requite; which went
Beyond all man's endeavours: my endeavours
Have ever come too short of my desires,
Yet filed with my abilities: mine own ends
Have been mine so that evermore they pointed
To the good of your most sacred person and
The profit of the state. For your great graces
Heap'd upon me, poor undeserver, I
Can nothing render but allegiant thanks,
My prayers to heaven for you, my loyalty,
Which ever has and ever shall be growing,
Till death, that winter, kill it.

King Henry
Fairly answer'd;
A loyal and obedient subject is
Therein illustrated.

Cardinal Wolsey
I do profess
That for your highness' good I ever labour'd
More than mine own; that am, have, and will be –
Though all the world should crack their duty to you,
And throw it from their soul; yet my duty,

As doth a rock against the chiding flood,
Should the approach of this wild river break,
And stand unshaken yours.

King Henry
'Tis nobly spoken:
Take notice, lords, he has a loyal breast,
For you have seen him open't. Read o'er this;

Giving him the papers he was previously reading.

And after, this: and then to breakfast with
What appetite you have.

Exit **King Henry**, *frowning upon* **Cardinal Wolsey**: *The Nobles throng after him.*

Smiling and whispering.

Cardinal Wolsey
What should this mean?
What sudden anger's this? how have I reap'd it?
He parted frowning from me, as if ruin
Leap'd from his eyes: so looks the chafed lion
Upon the daring huntsman that has gall'd him;
Then makes him nothing. I must read this paper;
I fear, the story of his anger. 'Tis so;
This paper has undone me: 'tis the account
Of all that world of wealth I have drawn together
For mine own ends; indeed, to gain the popedom,
And fee my friends in Rome. O negligence!
Is there no way to cure this?
No new device to beat this from his brains?
I know 'twill stir him strongly; yet I know
A way, if it take right, in spite of fortune
Will bring me off again. What's this? 'To the Pope!'
The letter, as I live, with all the business
I writ to's holiness. Nay then, farewell!
I have touch'd the highest point of all my greatness;
And, from that full meridian of my glory,
I haste now to my setting: I shall fall

Like a bright exhalation in the evening,
And no man see me more.

Re-enter **Norfolk** *and* **Surrey**, *and the* **Chamberlain** – *they undress* **Wolsey** *to his underwear as they speak.*

Norfolk
Hear the king's pleasure, cardinal: who commands you
To render up the great seal presently
Into our hands; and to confine yourself
To Asher House, my Lord of Winchester's,
Till you hear further from his highness.

Cardinal Wolsey
Stay:
Where's your commission, lords? words cannot carry
Authority so weighty.

Chamberlain
Who dare cross 'em,
Bearing the king's will from his mouth expressly?

Cardinal Wolsey
Till I find more than will or words to do it,
I mean your malice, know, officious lords,
I dare and must deny it. Now I feel
Of what coarse metal ye are moulded, envy:
How eagerly ye follow my disgraces,
As if it fed ye! and how sleek and wanton
Ye appear in every thing may bring my ruin!
Follow your envious courses, men of malice;
You have Christian warrant for 'em, and, no doubt,
In time will find their fit rewards. That seal,
You ask with such a violence, the king,
Mine and your master, with his own hand gave me;
Bade me enjoy it, with the place and honours,
During my life; and, to confirm his goodness,
Tied it by letters-patents: now, who'll take it?

Surrey
The king, that gave it.

Cardinal Wolsey
It must be himself, then.

Surrey
Thou art a proud traitor, priest.

Cardinal Wolsey
Proud lord, thou liest:
Within these forty hours Surrey durst better
Have burnt that tongue than said so.

Surrey
Thy ambition,
Thou scarlet sin, robb'd this bewailing land
Of noble Buckingham, my father-in-law:
The heads of all thy brother cardinals,
With thee and all thy best parts bound together,
Weigh'd not a hair of his. Plague of your policy!

Cardinal Wolsey
This, and all else
This talking lord can lay upon my credit,
I answer is most false. The duke by law
Found his deserts: how innocent I was
From any private malice in his end,

Surrey
By my soul,
Your long coat, priest, protects you; thou
shouldst feel
My sword i' the life-blood of thee else. My lords,
Can ye endure to hear this arrogance?
And from this fellow

Cardinal Wolsey
All goodness
Is poison to thy stomach.

Surrey
Yes, that goodness
Of gleaning all the land's wealth into one,

Into your own hands, cardinal, by extortion;
The goodness of your intercepted packets
You writ to the Pope against the king: your goodness,
Since you provoke me, shall be most notorious.
Now, if you can blush and cry 'guilty,' cardinal,
You'll show a little honesty.

Cardinal Wolsey
If I blush,
It is to see a nobleman want manners.

Surrey
I had rather want those than my head.

Chamberlain
Lord cardinal, the king's further pleasure is,
Because all those things you have done of late,
To forfeit all your goods, lands, tenements,
Chattels, and whatsoever, and to be
Out of the king's protection. This is my charge.

Norfolk
And so we'll leave you to your meditations
How to live better. For your stubborn answer
About giving back the great seal to us,
The king shall know it, and, no doubt, shall thank you.
So fare you well, my little good lord cardinal.

Exit all but **Cardinal Wolsey**, *leaving his clothes in a pile.*

Cardinal Wolsey
So farewell to the little good you bear me.
Farewell! A long farewell, to all my greatness!
This is the state of man: to-day he puts forth
The tender leaves of hopes; to-morrow blossoms,
And bears his blushing honours thick upon him;
The third day comes a frost, a killing frost,
And, when he thinks, good easy man, full surely
His greatness is a-ripening, nips his root,
And then he falls, as I do. I have ventured,
Like little wanton boys that swim on bladders,

This many summers in a sea of glory,
But far beyond my depth: my high-blown pride
At length broke under me and now has left me,
Weary and old with service, to the mercy
Of a rude stream, that must for ever hide me.
Vain pomp and glory of this world, I hate ye:
I feel my heart new open'd. O, how wretched
Is that poor man that hangs on princes' favours!
There is, betwixt that smile we would aspire to,
That sweet aspect of princes, and their ruin,
More pangs and fears than wars or women have:
And when he falls, he falls like Lucifer,
Never to hope again.

Enter **Cromwell**, *and stands amazed.*

Why, how now, Cromwell!

Cromwell
I have no power to speak, sir.

Cardinal Wolsey
What, amazed
At my misfortunes? can thy spirit wonder
A great man should decline? Nay, an you weep,
I am fall'n indeed.

Cromwell
How does your grace?

Cardinal Wolsey
Why, well;
Never so truly happy, my good Cromwell.
I know myself now; and I feel within me
A peace above all earthly dignities,
A still and quiet conscience. The king has cured me,
I humbly thank his grace; and from these shoulders,
These ruin'd pillars, out of pity, taken
A load would sink a navy, too much honour:
O, 'tis a burthen, Cromwell, 'tis a burthen
Too heavy for a man that hopes for heaven!

Cromwell
I am glad your grace has made that right use of it.

Cardinal Wolsey
I hope I have.
What news abroad?

Cromwell
The heaviest and the worst
Is your displeasure with the king.

Cardinal Wolsey
God bless him!

Cromwell
The next is, that Sir Thomas More is chosen
Lord Chancellor in your place.

Cardinal Wolsey
That's somewhat sudden:
But he's a learned man.
What more?

Cromwell
Last, that the Lady Anne,
Whom the king hath in secrecy long married,
This day was view'd in open as his queen,
Going to chapel; and the voice is now
Only about her coronation.

Cardinal Wolsey
There was the weight that pull'd me down. O Cromwell,
The king has gone beyond me: all my glories
In that one woman I have lost for ever:
Go, get thee from me, Cromwell;
I am a poor fall'n man, unworthy now
To be thy lord and master: seek the king;
That sun, I pray, may never set! I have told him
What and how true thou art: he will advance thee.

Cromwell
O my lord,

Must I, then, leave you? Must I needs forego
So good, so noble and so true a master?
Bear witness, all that have not hearts of iron,
With what a sorrow Cromwell leaves his lord.
The king shall have my service: but my prayers
For ever and for ever shall be yours.

Cardinal Wolsey

Cromwell, I charge thee, fling away ambition:
By that sin fell the angels;
Love thyself last:
Be just, and
Let all the ends thou aim'st at be thy country's,
Thy God's, and truth's;
Serve the king;
And, – prithee, lead me in:
There take an inventory of all I have,
To the last penny; 'tis the king's: my integrity to heaven, is
all I dare now call mine own. O Cromwell, Cromwell!
Had I but served my God with half the zeal
I served my king, he would not in mine age
Have left me naked to mine enemies.

Cromwell

Good sir, have patience.

Cardinal Wolsey

So I have. Farewell
The hopes of court! my hopes in heaven do dwell.

Exit **Wolsey**.

During this song the **King** *rips* **Wolsey**'s *clothes into pieces.*

The Visions *return and sing:*

How sour sweet music is
When time is broke and no proportion kept!
So is it in the music of men's lives.
And here have I the daintiness of ear
To check time broke in a disorder'd string;

But, for the concord of my state and time,
Had not an ear to hear my true time broke.
I wasted time, and now doth time waste me;
For now hath time made me his numb'ring clock:
My thoughts are minutes; and with sighs they jar
Their watches on unto mine eyes, the outward watch,
Whereto my finger, like a dial's point,
Is pointing still, in cleansing them from tears.
Now sir, the sound that tells what hour it is
Are clamorous groans which strike upon my heart,
Which is the bell. So sighs, and tears, and groans,
Show minutes, times, and hours.

They exit.

Act Four

Scene One

A street in Westminster.

Enter two Gentlewomen, meeting one another once more.

Woman One
You're well met once again.

Woman Two
So are you.

Woman One
You come to take your stand here, and behold
The Lady Anne pass from her coronation?

Woman Two
'Tis all my business. At our last encounter,
The Duke of Buckingham came from his trial.

Woman One
'Tis very true: but that time offer'd sorrow;
This, general joy.

Woman Two
'Tis well: the citizens,
I am sure, have shown at full their royal minds –
As, let 'em have their rights, they are ever forward –
In celebration of this day with shows,
Pageants and sights of honour.

Woman One
Never greater,
Nor, I'll assure you, better taken, madam.

Woman Two
May I be bold to ask at what that contains,
That paper in your hand?

Woman One

Yes; 'tis the list
Of those that claim their offices this day
By custom of the coronation.
The Duke of Surrey is the first, and claims
To be high-steward; next, the Duke of Norfolk,
He to be earl marshal: you may read the rest.

Woman Two

I thank you, madam: had I not known those customs,
I should have been beholding to your paper.
But, I beseech you, what's become of Katharine,
The princess dowager? How goes her business?

Woman One

That I can tell you too. The Archbishop
Of Canterbury, accompanied with other
Learned and reverend fathers of his order,
Held a late court at Dunstable,
And, to be short,
by the main assent
Of all these learned men she was divorced,
And the late marriage made of none effect
Since which she was removed to Kimbolton,
Where she remains now sick.

Woman Two

Alas, good lady and her daughter!

Woman One

Yes yes poor Mary, forbidden from seeing her mother.

Trumpets.

The trumpets sound: stand close, the new queen is
coming.

Hautboys.

The procession of Coronation passes over the stage.

Mary *is watching all this from the Musicians' gallery.*

Woman Two
A royal train, believe me. These I know:
Who's that that bears the sceptre?

Woman One
Marquess Dorset:
And that the Earl of Surrey, with the rod.

Woman Two
Heaven bless thee!

Looking on **Anne**.

Thou hast the sweetest face I ever look'd on.
madam, as I have a soul, she is an angel;
Our king has all the Indies in his arms,
And more and richer, when he strains that lady:
I cannot blame his conscience.

Woman One
They that bear
The cloth of honour over her, are four barons
Of the Cinque-ports.

Woman Two
Those men are happy; and so are all are near her.
I take it, she that carries up the train
Is that old noble lady, Duchess of Norfolk.

Woman One
It is; and all the rest are countesses.

Woman Two
Their coronets say so. These are stars indeed;
And sometimes falling ones.

Woman One
No more of that.

Indicating the audience are listening and may not approve of such talk.

GOD SAVE THE QUEEN is sung.

Now we watch **Anne** *being crowned –*

She leans forward with her neck exposed and the presence of a sword nearby in a way that should make us think about her fate to come.

As the crown is placed on her head she should look small and insignificant – barely able to hold herself up with the weight of the crown.

This done she stands and the procession exits, then a great flourish of trumpets.

Mary *is beside herself, she starts to make a scene. She screams the following and won't stop.*

Mary
GOD SAVE THE QUEEN – GOD SAVE HER!

Eventually she is dragged violently inside by several courtiers – she doesn't go willingly.

Enter a **Gentleman**.

Woman One
God save you, Sir! Where have you been broiling?

Gentleman
Among the crowd i' the Abbey; where a finger
Could not be wedged in more: I am stifled
With the mere rankness of their joy.

Woman Two
You saw
The ceremony?

Gentleman
That I did.

Woman One
How was it?

Gentleman
Well worth the seeing.
Such joy
I never saw before. Great-bellied women,
That had not half a week to go, like rams
In the old time of war, would shake the press,

And make 'em reel before 'em. No man living
Could say 'This is my wife' there; all were woven
So strangely in one piece.

Woman Two
But, what follow'd?

Gentleman
To York-place, where the feast is held.

Woman One
My Lord,
You must no more call it York-place, that's past;
For, since the cardinal fell, that title's lost:
'Tis now the king's, and call'd Whitehall.

Gentleman
I know it;
But 'tis so lately alter'd, that the old name
Is fresh about me.
Come, gentlewomen, ye shall go my way, which
Is to the court, and there ye shall be my guests:
Something I can command. As I walk thither,
I'll tell ye more.

Both Women
You may command us, Sir.

All Three
Let us go in together.

Exit.

Scene Two

Kimbolton.

Enter **Katharine**, *Dowager, sick; led by* **Patience**, *her woman.*
Katharine *holds a letter.*

Katharine
Patience! Deliver this to the King.

She hands her the letter.

Patience

How does your grace?

Katharine

O Patience, sick to death!
My daughter! O, my daughter! She takes
this going grievously.

Patience

As do you lady.

Katharine

My legs, like loaden branches, bow to the earth,
Willing to leave their burthen. Reach a chair:
So; now, methinks, I feel a little ease.
Didst thou not tell me, Patience, as thou led'st me,
That the great child of honour, Cardinal Wolsey, was
dead?

Patience

Yes, madam; but I think your grace,
Out of the pain you suffer'd, gave no ear to't.

Katharine

Prithee, good Patience, tell me how he died:
If well, he stepp'd before me, happily
For my example.

Patience

Well, the voice goes, madam:
He fell sick suddenly, and grew so ill
He could not sit his mule.
He died full of repentance,
Continual meditations, tears, and sorrows,
He gave his honours to the world again,
His blessed part to heaven, and slept in peace.

Katharine

So may he rest; his faults lie gently on him!

Patience

This cardinal,
Though from an humble stock, undoubtedly
Was fashion'd to much honour from his cradle.
He was a scholar, and a ripe and good one;
Exceeding wise, fair-spoken, and persuading:
Lofty and sour to them that loved him not;
But to those men that sought him sweet as summer.
His overthrow heap'd happiness upon him;
For then, and not till then, he felt himself,
And found the blessedness of being little:
And, to add greater honours to his age
Than man could give him, he died fearing God.

Katharine

After my death I wish no other herald,
No other speaker of my living actions,
To keep mine honour from corruption,
But such an honest chronicler as Patience.
Him whom I most hated living, thou hast made me,
With thy religious truth and modesty,
Now in his ashes honour: peace be with him!
Patience, be near me still; and set me lower:
I have not long to trouble thee. Good Patience,
Cause the musicians play me that sad note
I named my knell, whilst I sit meditating
On that celestial harmony I go to.

Patience

She is asleep: good wench, let's sit down quiet,
For fear we wake her:

The vision.

*Five women enter, they are **King Henry**'s wives to come. They are all wearing the same thing, they surround **Katharine** looking down on her kindly. They are like nurses, stroking her hair, calming and soothing her. **Katharine** sees them, she speaks to them – she needs them to understand.*

The Vision song

Sigh no more, ladies, sigh no more!
Men were deceivers ever,
One foot in sea, and one on shore;
To one thing constant never.
Then sigh not so,
But let them go,
And be you blithe and bonny,
Converting all your sounds of woe
Into Hey nonny, nonny.
Sing no more ditties, sing no moe,
Of dumps so dull and heavy!
The fraud of men was ever so,
Since summer first was leavy.
Then sigh not so,
But let them go,
And be you blithe and bonny,
Converting all your sounds of woe
Into Hey nonny, nonny.

Katharine

A more unhappy lady,
If this division chance, ne'er stood between,
Praying for both parts.
You ladies will mock me presently
When I shall pray 'O, bless my lord and husband!'

They hush and soothe her while repeating the following in a choral,
chanted, spell-like fashion several times over.

Vision One

All his faults observ'd,

Vision Two

Set in a note-book,

Vision Three

Learn'd and conn'd by rote,

Vision Four

To cast into my teeth.

Vision Five

O, I could weep My spirit from mine eyes!

They have reassured her somehow as they wipe her tears and leave.
The music continues.

Katharine

Spirits of peace, where are ye? are ye all gone,
And leave me here in wretchedness behind ye?

Patience

Madam, I am here.

Katharine

It is not you I call for:
Saw ye none enter since I slept?

Patience

None, madam.

Katharine

No? Saw you not, even now, a blessed troop
whose bright faces
Cast thousand beams upon me, like the sun?

Patience

I am most joyful, madam, such good dreams
Possess your fancy.

Katharine

Bid the music leave,
They are harsh and heavy to me.

Music ceases.

Patience

How much her grace is alter'd on the sudden?
How long her face is drawn? how pale she looks,
And of an earthy cold? Mark her eyes!

She is going,
Heaven comfort her!

Katharine
Mark you the letter Patience, for the King?

Patience
I will not forget it, or you my lady.

Katharine
I thank you, honest Maid. Remember me
In all humility unto his highness:
Say his long trouble now is passing
Out of this world; tell him, in death I bless'd him,
For so I will. *'O, bless my lord and husband!'*
Mine eyes grow dim. Farewell,
Nay, Patience,
You must not leave me yet: I must to bed;
Call in more women. When I am dead, good wench,
Let me be used with honour: strew me over
With maiden flowers, that all the world may know
I was a chaste wife to my grave: embalm me,
Then lay me forth: although unqueen'd, yet like
A queen, and daughter to a king, inter me.
I can no more.

Mary *enters and sings a song with* **Katharine**.

Come away, come away, death;
And in sad cypress let me be laid;
Fly away, fly away, breath,
I am slain by a fair cruel maid.
My shroud of white, stuck all with yew,
O, prepare it!
My part of death no one so true
Did share it.
Not a flower, not a flower sweet,
On my black coffin let there be strown;
Not a friend, not a friend greet
My poor corpse where my bones shall be thrown;

A thousand thousand sighs to save,
Lay me, O, where
Sad true lover never find my grave,
To weep there!

Katherine *exits.*

Mary *remains on stage for now.*

Act Five

Scene One

London. A gallery in the palace.

Anne *enters and speaks – as she does we watch her dress being filled to represent her pregnancy – we literally watch her grow the baby in front of our eyes – by the end of her speech she has gone into labour.*

Anne
Why not a mother? When I said 'a mother,'
Methought you saw a serpent. What's in 'mother'
That you start at it?
Youth's a stuff will not endure
Look in thy glass Anne, tell the face thou viewest,
Now is the time that face should form another,
Thou art thy mother's glass and she in thee
Calls back the lovely April of her prime,
So thou through windows of thine age shalt see,
Despite of wrinkles this thy golden time.
But die single and thine image dies with thee.

She screams as her labour begins.

Why not a mother?
Why not?
The world must be peopled.

Anne *is now in labour.*

She screams again.

Mary *puts her hands over her ears, trying to block out the sounds of her soon-to-be half-sister's birth. She runs off.*

*An attendant takes **Anne** behind a partition so we can no longer see her but throughout the scene we hear her pushing and panting. It should not be comic. We should be aware she may be in danger.*
Norfolk *and* **Surrey** *enter worried. They look at one another.*

Enter **King Henry**.

King Henry
Now, Norfolk, from the queen what is the news?

Norfolk
I could not personally deliver to her
What you commanded me, but by her woman
I sent your message; who return'd her thanks
In the great'st humbleness, and desired your highness
Most heartily to pray for her.

King Henry
What say'st thou, ha?
To pray for her? what, is she crying out?

Norfolk
So said her woman; and that her sufferance made
Almost each pang a death.

King Henry
Alas, good lady!

Surrey
God safely quit her of her burthen, and
With gentle travail, to the gladding of
Your highness with an heir!

King Henry
'Tis midnight, Lords;
Prithee, to bed; and in thy prayers remember
The estate of my poor queen. Leave me alone;
For I must think of that which company
Would not be friendly to.

Surrey
I wish your highness
A quiet night; and my good mistress will
Remember in my prayers.

King Henry
Lords good night.

Exit **Surrey** *and* **Norfolk**.

King Henry *stands for a moment. Then he takes the letter from*
Katharine *out of his pocket. He reads it aloud. The ghost of*
Katharine *(now dressed as the Visions were) watches from the upper*
gallery all in white. She speaks or mouths the words she wrote as he
says them.

King Henry
More letters – what now?

(He reads.)
  My most dear lord, king and husband,

  From Katharine . . .

  The hour of my death now drawing on, the tender love I owe you
  forceth me, my case being such, to commend myself to you, and to
  put you in remembrance with a few words of the health and
  safeguard of your soul which you ought to prefer before all worldly
  matters. For my part, I pardon you everything, and I wish to
  devoutly pray God that He will pardon you also.

  For the rest, I commend unto you our daughter Mary, beseeching
  you to be a good father unto her, as I have heretofore desired. I
  entreat you also, on behalf of my maids, to give them marriage
  portions. Lastly, I make this vow, that mine eyes desire you above
  all things.

  Katharine the Quene.

A beat.

  'be a good father unto her'

A beat.

Then a loud piercing cry from **Anne** *breaks the silence.* **King**
Henry *screws up the letter as he covers his ears in exactly the same*
way as **Mary** *did.*

He cannot bear the noise so calls his gentlemen back.

King Henry
Gentlemen – !

Surrey (*within*)
  Come back: what mean you?

Enter **Hope** *and* **Surrey**.

Hope
  I'll not come back; the tidings that I bring
  Will make my boldness manners. Now, good angels
  Fly o'er thy royal head, and shade thy person
  Under their blessed wings!

King Henry
  Now, by thy looks
  I guess thy message. Is the queen deliver'd?
  Say, ay; and of a boy.

Hope
  Ay, ay, my liege;
  And of a lovely boy: the God of heaven
  Both now and ever bless her! 'tis a girl,
  Promises boys hereafter.
  Sir, your queen
  Desires your visitation, and to be
  Acquainted with this stranger 'tis as like you
  As cherry is to cherry.

King Henry
  Surrey!

Surrey
  Sir?

King Henry
  Give her an hundred marks. I'll to the queen.

Exit.

Hope
  An hundred marks! By this light, I'll ha' more.
  An ordinary groom is for such payment.
  I will have more, or scold it out of him.
  Said I for this, the girl was like to him?

I will have more, or else unsay't; and now,
While it is hot, I'll put it to the issue.

Exit.

Scene Two

Noise and tumult within. A joyous song plays – perhaps an upbeat version of the Coronation song – and the audience are encouraged to clap and join in with the dance they were taught at the top of the show.

Enter **Porter** *and his woman through the yard trying to keep the groundlings under control as they make a way for the Royal procession.*

Porter
Christenings! You must be seeing Christenings!
You'll leave your noise anon, ye rascals: do you
take the court for Paris-garden? Ye rude slaves,
leave your gaping.
Is this a place to roar in? Fetch me a dozen crab-tree
staves, and strong ones: these are but switches to 'em. I'll
scratch your heads: you must be seeing christenings? Do
you look for ale and cakes here, you rude rascals?

Porter's Woman
Pray, sir, be patient: 'tis as much impossible –
Unless we sweep 'em from the door with cannons –
To scatter 'em, as 'tis to make 'em sleep
On May-day morning; which will never be:
We may as well push against Powle's, as stir em.

Porter
How got they in, and be hang'd?

Porter's Woman
Alas, I know not; how gets the tide in?
What would you have me do?

Porter

What should you do, but knock 'em down by the
dozens? Is this Moorfields to muster in?
Bless me, what a
fry of
is at door! On my Christian
conscience, this one christening will beget a
thousand; here will be father, godfather, and all together.

Porter's Woman

How now, woolsack? What mutter you? Why, you
whoreson round man, what's the matter? Zounds, ye fat
paunch, an ye call me coward, by the Lord, I'll stab thee.

Enter **Chamberlain** *on stage.*

Chamberlain

Mercy o' me, what a multitude are here!
They grow still too; from all parts they are coming,
As if we kept a fair here! Where are these porters,
These lazy knaves? Ye have made a fine hand, fellows:
There's a trim rabble let in: are all these
Your faithful friends o' the suburbs? We shall have
Great store of room, no doubt, left for the ladies,
When they pass back from the christening.

Porter

An't please
your honour,
We are but men;

Porter's Woman

And women!

Porter

and what so many may do,
Not being torn a-pieces, we have done:
An army cannot rule 'em.

Chamberlain

As I live,
If the king blame me for't, I'll lay ye all

By the heels, and suddenly; and on your heads
Clap round fines for neglect: ye are lazy knaves;
And here ye lie baiting of bombards, when
Ye should do service. Hark! the trumpets sound;
They're come already from the christening:
Go, break among the press, and find a way out
To let the troop pass fairly; or I'll find
A Marshalsea shall hold ye play these two months.

Porter
Make way there for the princess.

Porter's Woman
You great fellow,
Stand close up, or I'll make your head ache.

Porter
You i' the camlet, get up o' the rail;
I'll peck you o'er the pales else.

Enter the Christening procession which includes **King Henry**,
Anne *and* **Cromwell** *and baby* **Elizabeth**, *plus* **Cromwell** *and*
Chamberlain.

Chamberlain
Heaven, from thy endless goodness, send prosperous
life, long, and ever happy, to the high and mighty
princess of England, Elizabeth!

Flourish.

Enter **King Henry** *and Guard.*

Cromwell (*kneeling*)
And to your royal grace, and the good queen,
My noble partners, and myself, thus pray:
All comfort, joy, in this most gracious lady,
Heaven ever laid up to make parents happy,
May hourly fall upon ye!

King Henry
Thank you,
What is her name?

Cromwell
Elizabeth.

King Henry
Stand up, lord.

King Henry *kisses the child.*

With this kiss take my blessing: God protect thee!
Into whose hand I give thy life.
My noble gossips, ye have been too prodigal:
I thank ye heartily; so shall this lady,
When she has so much English.

*As **Cromwell** describes **Elizabeth** she enters as a fully grown
woman to the Musicians' gallery. Her attendants dress her and
transform her into the Queen we know from portraits. They fix jewels
on her and complete her make-up. They have departed by the end of
Cromwell*'s speech.*

Cromwell
Let me speak, sir,
This royal infant – heaven still move about her! –
Though in her cradle, yet now promises
Upon this land a thousand thousand blessings,
Which time shall bring to ripeness: she shall be –
But few now living can behold that goodness –
A pattern to all princes living with her,
And all that shall succeed:
truth shall nurse her,
Holy and heavenly thoughts still counsel her:
She shall be loved and fear'd: her own shall bless her;
Her foes shake like a field of beaten corn,
And hang their heads with sorrow: good grows with her:
In her days every man shall eat in safety,
Under his own vine, what he plants; and sing
The merry songs of peace to all his neighbours:

She shall be, to the happiness of England,
An aged princess; many days shall see her,
And yet no day without a deed to crown it.
Would I had known no more! but she must die,
She must, the saints must have her; yet a virgin,
A most unspotted lily shall she pass
To the ground, and all the world shall mourn her.

They all turn and look at **Elizabeth**.

Anne
By my troth and maidenhead I would not be Queen.

Baby Elizabeth *begins to cry in her cot – as though she knows everything that is to come.*

Mary *enters and looks at the crib – she picks up the baby, what will she do?*

After a moment considering her baby sister, she hands her to their father who looks totally uncomfortable holding her. Still she cries. He hands the baby to her mother and exits. **Anne** *gazes at her daughter lovingly.*

Anne
Did my heart love til now?

Still the baby cries.

Canst thou, O partial sleep, give thy repose
To the wet sea-boy in an hour so rude;
And in the calmest and most stillest night,
With all appliances and means to boot,
Deny it to a Princess? Then, happy low, lie down!

Anne, **Elizabeth** *and* **Mary**
Uneasy lies the head that wears a crown.

All exit and leave **Elizabeth** *alone on stage.*

Then **Elizabeth** *addresses the audience.*

Elizabeth
To be a King, and were a Crown, is a thing more glorious
to them that see it, than it is pleasant to them that bear it:

for my selfe, I never was so much inticed with the glorious
name of a King, or the royal authority of a Queen, as
delighted that God hath made Me his Instrument to
maintain his Truth and Glory, and to defend this Kingdom
from dishonor, damage, tyranny, and oppression. The
cares and trouble of a Crown I cannot more fitly resemble,
than to the Drugges of a learned Physitian, perfumed with
some Aromatical savour, or to bitter pills gilded over, by
which they are made more acceptable or lesse offensive,
which indeed are bitter and unpleasant to take; and for
mine own part, were it not for conscience sake to
discharge the duty that God hath laid upon Me, & to
maintain his Glory, and keep you in Safety, in mine own
disposition I should be willing to resigne the place I hold
to any other, and glad to be freed of the Glory with the
Labors: For it is not my desire to live or reign longer, than
my life & reign shall be for your good. And though you
have had and may have many mightier and wiser Princes
sitting in this Seat, yet you never had, nor shall have any
that will love you better.

A canon goes off.

The company rushes on and looks up . . . is there smoke?

Ends.

Printed in the USA
CPSIA information can be obtained
at www.ICGtesting.com
LVHW020940020923
756969LV00009B/422